"A searing and provocative critique of our growth-based oil economy. Stan Cox suggests remedies that should ignite lively discussion and intense debate, which is sorely needed. A must-read for those who care about our shared planetary future."

—Mary Evelyn Tucker, Senior Lecturer and Research Scholar at Yale School of Forestry and Environmental Studies, and co-author of *Journey of the Universe*

"Stan Cox isn't just another member of the chorus speaking truth to power about climate change. He has the courage, intelligence and resolve in this vital book to speak truth to the half-formed plans that are currently being offered as a balm to the crisis. The difficult truth is that there's going to need to be radical change in the way we all live our lives. With analysis as crystal clear as his prose, Cox explains why. His is a warning well worth heeding, and sharing, while we still have time."

—Raj Patel, co-author of *A History of the World in Seven Cheap Things: A Guide to Capitalism, Nature, and the Future of the Planet*

"In *The Green New Deal and Beyond*, Stan Cox presents a smart, sane, and plausibly optimistic alternative to abandoning all hope."

—David Owen, author of *Volume Control: Hearing in a Deafening World*

"Change is inevitable. The question is *who controls the change*. Indigenous Peoples' covenant with Mother Earth was the original Green Deal, yet our communities have been laid to waste by the economics of the Wiindigo—the monster of settler colonialism. For too long, we've relinquished control over our future to corporations and governments that have brought us to the present crisis. Across the world, people with vision, hope, and commitment are making plans and building infrastructure for our future. The teachings of Indigenous Peoples are still here, and it's up to the present generation to muster the courage and resources to follow those instructions. Stan Cox reminds us of this historic dialogue and development of the Green New Deal, and helps us find the path back to those instructions."

—Winona LaDuke (Anishinaabe), is author of many books, including *All Our Relations: Native Struggles for Land and Life* and *LaDuke Chronicles*

"If we as a species are going to survive climate change, we need a plan that is urgent, imaginative, and actionable. On most days, that struggle can feel hopeless. But reading Stan Cox and *The Green New Deal and Beyond*—analysis that's both innovative and pragmatic—it's hard not to feel like we just might have a fighting chance. An invaluable contribution to what must become an unprecedented international revolution."

—Will Potter, author of *Green Is the New Red: An Insider's Account of a Social Movement Under Siege*

"Stan Cox makes the rare but much needed point that if the economic system can't tolerate our doing what is necessary to prevent ecological breakdown, then it's the system that needs to be changed. He speaks with clarity and historical grounding about the fact that half measures will still take us off a cliff, yet follows with what can—and must—be done. Be inspired, and support what must happen to create conditions conducive to life. A low-energy society will lead us closer to peace and a healthy, sustainable planet."

—Jodie Evans, co-founder CODEPINK and board chair Rainforest Action Network

"I found *How the World Breaks* intriguing and unexpected in how it uses major disasters to illuminate inequalities of both wealth and power—and cases where a society acted wisely."

—Adam Hochschild, author of
Spain in Our Hearts and other books

"Think climate change is a far off, distant threat? Then think again. In their must-read new book *How the World Breaks*, father and son team Stan and Paul Cox travel the world exploring how the devastating impacts of disasters are made notably worse by human-caused climate change."

—Michael E. Mann, distinguished professor, Penn State University,
and author of *The Hockey Stick and the Climate Wars*

"A devastating account of how regular working people show great bravery and generosity in the face of disaster, but also how the sheer number of disasters can overwhelm a society's ability to recover."

—Erik Loomis, author of *Out of Sight*

"With powerful prose and meticulous scrutiny, *How the World Breaks* strips naked the dynamics of risk creation and the consequent disasters. Alternating chapters of keen analysis and veracious case studies elucidate the false notion that disasters bring about beneficial change, demonstrate who profits as opposed to who pays the price, and illuminate how failed disaster policies have led to horrific duress. A must-read for everyone in all the fields relating to disaster studies, and indeed all who are asking what is breaking apart the world today."

—Dr. Susanna Hoffman, editor of *The Angry Earth*
and *Catastrophe and Culture*

"A breathtaking new view of crisis and recovery on the unstable landscapes of the Earth's hazard zones."

—Resilience.org

PRAISE FOR *ANY WAY YOU SLICE IT* (2013)

"An iconoclast of the best kind, Stan Cox has an all-too-rare commitment to following arguments wherever they lead, however politically dangerous that turns out to be. In this richly informative and deeply courageous book, he tackles one of the greatest taboos of our high-consumer culture: the need to consume less and to fairly share what's left."

—Naomi Klein

"Today, rationing is about as acceptable a topic of conversation as hemorrhoids. But that doesn't mean it isn't happening. In fact, we do it every day, and our reluctance to admit it serves us poorly. From death panels to water wars, *Any Way You Slice It* explains with wit and sophistication how rationing happens. More important, Stan Cox gives us the tools to talk about rationing sensibly. And if we heed him, those conversations will not only be better informed, but might even lead to a better democracy."

—Raj Patel, author of *The Value of Nothing*

"A cool and cogent analysis of a taboo subject . . . a brilliant opening of a global dialogue on who gets what, when, why, and how."

—David W. Orr, Paul Sears Professor of Environmental Studies and Politics, Oberlin College

"The warning signs are flashing ominously everywhere you turn: warming climate, swelling populations, dwindling water supplies, rising food costs, a host of new deadly diseases, and a widening chasm between the super-rich and the destitute. The ecological crisis afflicting the planet has mutated into a savage political and economic crisis that threatens to erode the very foundations of human culture. Time is running out for incremental, piecemeal solutions to these looming global threats. In *Any Way You Slice It*, Stan Cox offers a way out through a kind of ethical and rational triage. He maps out a plan to ration the Earth's shrinking resources in a way that is socially just and ecologically sane. This brave book is not for the timid or those frozen by political taboos, but it is a must-read for those who want to forge real change before the ecological doomsday clock strikes midnight."

—Jeffrey St. Clair, author of *Born Under a Bad Sky*

PRAISE FOR *LOSING OUR COOL* (2010)

"Well-written, thoroughly researched, with a truly global focus, the book offers much for consumers, environmentalists, and policy makers to consider before powering up to cool down."

—*Publishers Weekly*

"Important. . . . What I like about Cox's book is that he isn't an eco-nag or moralist."

—Tom Condon, *Hartford Courant*

"Stan Cox offers both some sobering facts and some interesting strategies for thinking through a big part of our energy dilemma."

—Bill McKibben

"This is an important book. The history of air-conditioning is really the history of the world's energy and climate crises, and by narrowing the focus Stan Cox makes the big picture comprehensible. He also suggests remedies—which are different from the ones favored by politicians, environmentalists, and appliance manufacturers, not least because they might actually work."

—David Owen, author of *Green Metropolis*

"As Stan Cox details in his excellent new book, *Losing Our Cool*, air conditioning has been a major force in shaping western society."

—Bradford Plumer, *The National*

"This book is the go-to source for a better understanding of the complexity of pumping cold air into a warming climate."

—Maude Barlow

THE
GREEN
NEW DEAL
and
BEYOND

THE
GREEN
NEW DEAL
and
BEYOND

Ending the Climate Emergency
While We Still Can

STAN COX

Foreword by Noam Chomsky

City Lights Books | Open Media Series
San Francisco

Open Media Series Editor: Greg Ruggiero

Cover design: Victor Mingovits

Library of Congress Cataloging-in-Publication Data
Names: Cox, Stan, author. | Chomsky, Noam, author of foreword.
Title: The green new deal and beyond : ending the climate emergency while
    we still can / Stan Cox ; forward by Noam Chomsky.
Description: San Francisco, CA : City Lights Books, 2020. | Series: Open
    media series | Includes bibliographical references.
Identifiers: LCCN 2020003318 | ISBN 9780872868069 (trade paperback)
Subjects: LCSH: Environmentalism—United States. | Environmental
    policy—United States. | Energy policy—United States. | Greenhouse
    gases—Government policy—United States. | Renewable energy
    sources—Government policy—United States.
Classification: LCC GE197 .C48 2020 | DDC 363.738/74560973—dc23
LC record available at https://lccn.loc.gov/2020003318

City Lights Books are published at the City Lights Bookstore
261 Columbus Avenue, San Francisco, CA 94133
www.citylights.com

CONTENTS

For Brenda Cox

FOREWORD

BY NOAM CHOMSKY

This essay is based on interviews with Chomsky conducted by C.J. Polychroniou, Amy Goodman, and Harrison Samphir.

History is all too rich in records of horrendous wars, indescribable torture, massacres, and every imaginable abuse of fundamental rights. But the threat of destruction of organized human life in any recognizable or tolerable form—that is entirely new. The environmental crisis under way is indeed unique in human history, and is a true existential crisis. Those alive today will decide the fate of humanity—and the fate of the other species that we are now destroying at a rate not seen for 65 million years, when a huge asteroid hit Earth, ending the age of the dinosaurs and opening the way for some small mammals to evolve to pose a similar threat to life as that earlier asteroid, though differing from it in that we can make a choice.

Meanwhile, the world watches as we proceed toward a catastrophe of unimaginable proportions. We are approaching perilously close to the global temperatures of 120,000 years ago, when sea levels were six to nine meters higher than today. Glaciers are sliding into the sea five times faster than in the 1990s, with over 100 meters of ice thickness lost in some areas due to ocean warming, and current losses doubling every decade. Complete loss of the ice sheets would raise sea levels by about five meters, drowning coastal cities, and with utterly devastating effects elsewhere—the low-lying plains of Bangladesh, for example.

This is only one of the many concerns of those who are paying attention to what is happening before our eyes.

Climate scientists are certainly paying close attention, and issuing dire warnings. "Things are getting worse," says Petteri Taalas, Secretary General of the World Meteorological Organization, which in December 2019 issued its annual global climate report. "It's more urgent than ever to proceed with mitigation. The only solution is to get rid of fossil fuels in power production, industry and transportation," he said.[1] Israeli climatologist Baruch Rinkevich captures the general mood succinctly:

> After us, the deluge, as the saying goes. People don't fully understand what we're talking about here. . . . They think about melting icebergs and polar bears who won't have a home. They don't understand that everything is expected to change: the air we breathe, the food we eat, the water we drink, the landscapes we see, the oceans, the seasons, the daily routine, the quality of life. Our children will have to adapt or become extinct. They will have to dress differently, behave differently, live differently. That's not for me. I'm happy I won't be here.[2]

Is there a chance to avoid such catastrophes? No doubt. There are well-worked-out and sound proposals, but the task ahead is enormous, and there is not much time. The challenge would be great even if states were committed to overcoming it. Some are. But it is impossible to overlook the fact that the most powerful state in human history is under the leadership of what can only be accurately described as a gang of criminals who are dedicated to racing to the cliff with abandon.

It is hard even to find words to capture the scale of the crimes they are contemplating. A small but telling example is a 500-page environmental assessment produced by President Trump's National Highway Traffic Safety Administration that calls for cancelling new automotive emissions standards. They have a sound argument. The study projects that by the end of the century temperatures will have risen 4 degrees Centigrade. Auto emissions don't add that much, and since the game is pretty much over, why not have fun while we can—fiddling while the planet burns.

We face a problem that cannot be ignored. The French *gilets jaunes* movement has put the problem squarely: The (French) government talks of the end of the world, but we can't get to the end of the month. Transition to renewable energy should create a much more livable environment quite generally, but it will inevitably harm some working people who can ill afford the shock, and careful planning is necessary to deal with these and many other problems. That can be done, and concrete solutions have been suggested.

The Green New Deal moves us in the right direction. You can raise questions about the specific form in which Alexandria Ocasio-Cortez and Ed Markey introduced it. But the general idea is quite right. And there's very solid work explaining exactly how it could work. For example, a very fine economist at University of Massachusetts, Amherst, Robert Pollin, has written extensively on it, and in extensive detail, with close analysis of how you could implement policies of this kind in a very effective way, which would actually make a better society. It wouldn't be that you'd lose from it; you'd gain from it. The costs of renewable energy are declining very sharply. If you eliminate the massive subsidies that are given to fossil fuels, renewable energy is probably already more cost-effective. There are many means that can be implemented and carried out to mitigate, maybe to overcome, this serious crisis. So the basic idea of the GND is, I think, completely defensible—in fact, essential.

Well, what's the difference between the Green New Deal of today and the New Deal from the 1930s? Several things. One thing that's different is large-scale labor action. The 1930s were the period of the organization of the CIO (Congress for Industrial Organization). In the 1920s, the U.S. labor movement had been virtually destroyed. Remember, this is very much a business-run society. American labor history is very violent, quite unlike comparable countries'. And by the 1920s, the quite effective, militant labor movement had been pretty much crushed. One of the great works of labor history is called *The Fall of the House of Labor: The Workplace, the State, and American Labor Activism, 1865–1925*, written by David Montgomery, one of the great labor historians. Montgomery was talking about the 1920s, when labor activism had essentially been destroyed. During the 1930s, it revived.

It revived with large-scale organizing activities. The CIO organizing began. The strike actions were quite militant. They led to sitdown strikes. A sitdown strike is a real sign of warning to the business classes, because there's a step beyond a sitdown strike. The next step beyond a sitdown strike is: "Let's start the factory by running it by ourselves. We don't need the bosses. We can run it ourselves. So, get rid of them. OK?" That's a real revolution, the kind that should take place. The participants in an enterprise would own and run it by themselves, instead of being the slaves of the private owners who control their lives. And a sitdown strike is a bare step away from that. That aroused real fear among the ownership classes.

The second element was there was a sympathetic administration, which is very critical. In his book *A History of America in Ten Strikes*, an account of the militant labor actions since the early 19th century, Erik Loomis makes an interesting point. He says every successful labor action has had at least tacit support of the government. When the government and the ownership classes have unified in crushing labor action, they've always succeeded. This is a very significant observation. And in the 1930s, there was a sympathetic administration, for many reasons. But that combination of militant labor action and a sympathetic administration did lead to the New Deal, which greatly changed people's lives.

Today, we know there are barriers that have to be overcome. We have to find ways to shape the message, in words and actions, so as to overcome the barriers. The message is two-fold: First, we're facing an existential crisis that must be dealt with quickly; and second, there are ways to overcome it.

The first part is expressed simply enough in current articles in the most prestigious and reliable journals. Oxford professor of physics Raymond Pierrehumbert, a lead author of the recent report from the IPCC (Intergovernmental Panel on Climate Change), opens his review of existing circumstances and options by writing: "Let's get this on the table right away, without mincing words. With regard to the climate crisis, yes, it's time to panic. . . . We are in deep trouble." He then lays out the details carefully and scrupulously, reviewing the possible technical fixes and their very serious problems, concluding, "There's no plan B." We must move to zero net carbon emissions, and fast.

Moving to zero net carbon emissions, and fast, is the point of Stan Cox's important new study, *The Green New Deal and Beyond*. Cox advocates on behalf of the GND as one step of several we need to take to stabilize the planet. But as Cox and others point out, the GND does not challenge the fossil-fuel industry. In fact, the term "fossil fuels" appears nowhere in the Congressional GND resolutions, and the GND think tanks are not stressing the elimination of fossil fuels. Cox suggests policies that would free us from fossil fuel use before it's too late. He also suggests doing so in a manner that breaks the patterns of social, racial, and environmental injustice that have been historically inseparable from the forms of economic injustice that have destabilized the planet's ecosystem.

There are also fundamental issues of value: What is a decent life? Should the master-servant relation be tolerated? Should one's goals really be maximization of commodities—Veblen's "conspicuous consumption"? Surely there are higher and more fulfilling aspirations. The dramatic actions of such groups as Extinction Rebellion, the Sunrise Movement, and School Strike for Climate are of great value in opening minds—but those minds have to be engaged in unremitting action to implement changes on the ground, to pass legislation like the Green New Deal, to educate and organize to move beyond it to phase out fossil fuels by a clear and definitive date.

The task will not be easy. It must be undertaken, urgently.

INTRODUCTION

Thanks to human-induced greenhouse warming, the Earth's average temperature today is about 1.2°C (2.2°F) higher than it was in the pre-fossil-fuel era. The Intergovernmental Panel on Climate Change (IPCC)[3] reported in 2018 that if warming is allowed to surpass 1.5°C, the world will risk widespread ecological destruction and human suffering. To keep temperatures below that limit, they concluded, global greenhouse emissions would have to be cut almost in half before 2030, and net-zero emissions would have to be achieved by 2050.[4] The United Nations' 2019 Emissions Gap Report projected that the world is on course for a catastrophic 3.2°C of warming by the end of this century. To hold warming to 1.5°, the report said, will require that global greenhouse emissions, which have been rising by 1.5 percent annually over the past decade, turn around immediately and start falling at the precipitous rate of 7.6 percent per year.[5]

Since 2018, climate groups in the United States have been pushing for a Green New Deal, a plan that calls for cutting net U.S. greenhouse emissions to zero through a just transition to an economy that runs on non-fossil energy. The still-evolving plan has given the climate movement a big shot in the arm, providing a sweeping national policy initiative that millions now regard as something worth rallying around. In that, the Green New Deal is part of a long tradition. The women's suffrage movement, the civil rights struggle, the movement to end the Vietnam War, the nuclear freeze of the 1980s, and the fight for reproductive choice have all focused on big demands: groundbreaking national legislation, concrete policy changes, or robust reinforcement of Constitutional rights. The Green New Deal has revived interest in public planning, and the kind of massive investment that can secure basic needs, including energy, for all. It has eclipsed previously popular half- and quarter-measures that would have only nibbled around the edges of the climate crisis. It has inspired vigorous resistance to the Trump administration's obsessively pro-fossil-fuel, anti-ecological policies. It has explicitly linked the need for climate mitigation to the need for social and racial justice, inclusion, and workers' power. It intends to shift the economic center of gravity away from the owning and investing classes toward those who do the nation's work. Those visionary features have not only positioned the Green New Deal at the heart of the climate movement, but have also earned support for it from a host of other movements, institutions, networks, scientists, and scholars.

In the pages that follow, I will present my case that the Green New Deal vision, ambitious as it is, must go even further and deeper. As the plan is formulated and carried out in coming months and years, it must be accompanied by effective mechanisms to (1) directly eliminate fossil fuels from the economy on an accelerated schedule and (2) reverse the widespread ecological damage that has been done in the pursuit of economic growth—damage that reaches well beyond greenhouse warming. Fossil fuels cannot be suppressed solely through the expansion of non-fossil energy or through market interventions such as carbon pricing; eradicating emissions will require a statutory limit on all fuel extraction, one that lowers quickly year by year, along with a system to guarantee material sufficiency for all people and excess for none. And even if we manage to free ourselves from fossil fuels, the reversal of broader ecological damage will not be achieved solely by the reduction or elimination of greenhouse emissions; it will require a transformed economy that operates on less, not more, energy and does not depend on over-exploitation of the Earth's ecosystems. I will also show why neither fossil-fuel elimination nor ecological restoration is compatible with continued economic growth.

DIRECT ACTION NEEDED

Deep social change cannot be achieved by a single piece of legislation, no matter how profound it is. An obvious example is the 1964 Civil Rights Act. It became essential because the Thirteenth and Fourteenth Amendments a century earlier had failed to end racial oppression. But the Civil Rights Act itself needed some backup. To be effective, it had to be followed up by the Voting Rights Act of 1965, the Fair Housing Act of 1968, and other major legislation—and that struggle is still not over. Passage of a Green New Deal, like that of the Civil Rights Act, is widely viewed as a vital step toward righting a wrong that threatens the nation. Nevertheless, one act of Congress cannot successfully tackle a multifaceted threat such as the emerging climate emergency. Like the Civil Rights Act, a Green New Deal Act can be the beginning of a transformation, but it can't be the end; it must be accompanied by other essential legislation.

The Green New Dealers have not yet specified a mechanism by which the United States can guarantee the elimination of greenhouse emissions by a hard-and-fast deadline. The absence of a direct, airtight mechanism to achieve the necessarily rapid decline and elimination of fossil fuels is not unique to the Green New Deal. None of the climate proposals debated so far, either in Washington or at international climate talks, have included such a component. But the intensifying symptoms of our climate predicament now require an immediate switch from the current steady rise in fossil-fuel use to a much steeper decline—something like doing a U-turn at 80 miles an hour in a tanker truck. There's no time left for legislating corporate-friendly policies and waiting to see if they work. If, in 2030 or 2040, such policies turn out to have been insufficient, it will be too late for a do-over.

The most widely discussed emissions-reduction strategies depend on three general elements: building up "green" energy capacity and infrastructure (with, in the case of the Green New Deal, lots of public investment); seeking to maintain or accelerate economic growth without increasing energy demand; and intervening in the market by setting a price on carbon in the event that greenhouse emissions are not declining fast enough.

If we are to eliminate fossil fuels from our society, the development of non-fossil energy capacity, as called for by the Green New Deal will be urgently needed. The national climate discussion, however, appears to be based on an implicit assumption that as new energy capacity comes online in the coming decade or two, it will push an equal quantity of fossil-energy capacity off-line. History and research argue against that assumption, showing that with economic growth, new energy sources simply add to the existing energy supply rather than replace it.[6]

The idea that investment in solar and wind technology and green infrastructure can work its way through the market to automatically eliminate fossil-fuel use and emissions is not supported by the evidence. So various interventions have been suggested to give new energy sources a leg up in the market. For example, governments could tax each of the fossil fuels based on the carbon emissions it produces; require energy companies to buy permits to burn or sell fossil fuels; or provide homeowners and business owners incentives to produce or buy solar or wind energy. Governmental and grassroots approaches to making fossil fuels more scarce or expensive include eliminating subsidies to the coal and petroleum industries; pressuring institutional investors to disinvest from those industries; banning leases and drilling on public land; and pressuring the industry through direct action, as with the anti-pipeline and "Keep It in the Ground" movements.

Most of these actions have been pursued in one or more places around the world. Worthy as they may be, all are at best indirect approaches to driving down carbon emissions. Research tells us, as I show in Chapter Three, that none of those approaches, separately or together, can make that necessary 80 mph U-turn. None of the widely debated climate strategies has included an element that is essential for fairly and humanely stopping greenhouse emissions: a mandatory, impervious cap on the quantities of fossil fuels entering the economy, one that lowers year by year, and is accompanied by planned allocation of the nation's energy resources and fair-share rationing of energy. I will outline how this might be done in Chapter Four.

The Green New Deal is a stimulus package in both name and aim. If not implemented with great care, it will encourage the same pursuit of economic growth that got us into this climate predicament in the first place.[7] Resource use must be carefully restrained during the transition; otherwise, the new non-fossil energy coming online will feed growth rather than displace oil, natural gas, and coal. (I generally avoid the term "renewable energy," because a wind turbine or solar array is not self-renewing in the way a forest or prairie is. But I will sometimes use the term when referring to others' documents or remarks.) Full displacement of fossil energy by non-fossil energy can happen only if a cap is imposed on fossil fuels, and that cap is lowered each year in order to eliminate their emissions on schedule. Even an urgent buildup of new energy capacity cannot proceed quickly enough to compensate for all of the fossil-fueled capacity being withdrawn, so our society will need to operate on a smaller total energy supply. The national economy will need to reorient toward ensuring sufficiency for all rather than feeding the accumulation of wealth by the few.

Successfully enacting such a system will not be easy, and time is running out. As the struggle for the Green New Deal and other legislation proceeds, there will be much wrangling over the question of what is politically acceptable. That's inevitable, but we must keep at the center of the public debate the most urgent question of all: What actions must be undertaken to eliminate greenhouse emissions in time?

THE DANGERS OF INACTION

The IPCC's 2018 report calls for a stepped-up rate of emissions reductions and highlights the devastating impacts expected if warming is allowed to rise past 1.5°C.[8] Letting the global temperature blow up to 2° or beyond would, says the report, risk irreversible loss of the Greenland and West Antarctic ice sheets, eventually raising sea levels by one to two meters. At 2°, one-fourth to over one-half of all permafrost will disappear, irreversibly releasing a surge of stored carbon into the atmosphere. Storms, wildfires, and pest outbreaks will cause far more widespread forest dieback at 2°, especially in Central and South America, the Mediterranean Basin, South Africa, and South Australia. The report expresses "high confidence" that warming of 2°

would generally increase the number of species extinctions, and the "irreversible loss of many marine and coastal ecosystems" in particular. Between 70 and 90 percent of coral reefs will be lost at 1.5°; at 2°, virtually all will die off.

The IPCC cites evidence suggesting that if we allow temperatures to rise from 1.5°C to 2°, the percentage of the world population exposed to severe heat waves in at least one out of five years would rise from 14 percent to 37 percent, affecting an increase of 1.7 billion people. An additional 420 million more people will be "frequently exposed to extreme heat waves," and about 65 million additional people will be exposed to "exceptional heatwaves," facing prolonged high temperatures that have only occurred very rarely up to now.[9]

The IPCC also projects a tenfold increase, to 362 million, in the number of people suffering crop loss and an almost eightfold increase, to 680 million, in the number living with severe habitat degradation if warming reaches 2°C. The number of people suffering increased water scarcity will increase by 184 million to 270 million. The number likely to experience flooding at 1.5° will be double the number subjected to flooding in the period from 1976 to 2005, and warming of 2° will expose an additional 26 to 34 million. The average monthly number of people exposed to extreme drought will rise globally from 114 million at 1.5° to 190 million at 2°.

The report projects that global warming and the food shortages that result[10] will increase the rate of childhood undernutrition, stunting, and mortality, particularly in Asia and Africa, and that the undernourished population will be much larger globally at 2°C than at 1.5°. Incidence of malaria will increase, and the geographic reach of the *Anopheles* mosquito will be extended. Ditto for the *Aedes* mosquito, which carries dengue fever, chikungunya, yellow fever, and the Zika virus. Also, according to the IPCC: "Most projections conclude that climate change could expand the geographic range and seasonality of Lyme and other tick-borne diseases in parts of North America and Europe."

The bad news doesn't stop there. The IPCC projects unprecedented waves of human migration: "Tropical populations may have to move distances greater than 1,000 km if global mean temperature rises by 2°. . . . A disproportionately rapid evacuation from the tropics could lead to a concentration of population in tropical margins and the sub-tropics, where population densities could increase by 300 percent or more." If warming exceeds 2°C by 2050, "rates of human conflict could increase." Going from 1.5° to 2° could increase the numbers of people susceptible to poverty "by up to several hundred million by 2050." And "populations at disproportionately higher risk of adverse conse-quences . . . include disadvantaged and vulnerable populations, some indigenous peoples, and local communities dependent on agricultural or coastal livelihoods."

The horrific wildfire emergency in Australia and deadly flooding in Jakarta, Indonesia, that ushered in the year 2020 demonstrated that for parts of the Earth, the nightmare future is already here, well before the 1.5°C global temperature rise. A 1.5° hotter world, when it arrives, will be an even tougher one to live in, and it appears inevitable at this point, according to IPCC. A 2° hotter world would clearly be catastrophic and must be avoided. The climate policies we adopt can't simply rely on green technology and high hopes to carry us into the future. They must be designed to directly and reliably minimize the risk of surpassing a 1.5° increase in global temperature. It is far more important to steer clear of a nightmare future than to strive for an idealized one.

THE POSSIBILITY OF A BETTER WORLD

Legislation for direct, rapid, and equitable elimination of fossil fuels, along with ecological renewal that goes beyond climate mitigation, will be keys to achieving the Green New Deal's vision. Its plans for urgently needed economic and social policies to create jobs, workers' and union rights and benefits, inclusive economic justice, guarantees of living wages and health care coverage, Indigenous rights, and vision for an end to racial oppression are all much-needed breakthroughs and are crucial for creating a genuinely more just society. The Green New Deal is forthright in recognizing that market forces would be sorely deficient in addressing the climate emergency, and its necessarily ambitious goals for the elimination of greenhouse emissions are achievable if Congress also takes tough action to stop the extraction and use of fossil fuels, by law and on schedule. Keeping fossil fuels buried in the Earth's crust will complement the Green New Deal's energy and justice proposals, rather than competing with them.

The promise of a Green New Deal resonates with an enormous and growing number of people. When, in 2019, *The Intercept* and Naomi Klein presented a seven-minute film called *A Message from the Future with Alexandria Ocasio-Cortez,*[11] it garnered 2 million views within eight hours of being posted. Written by Congresswoman Ocasio-Cortez (D-N.Y.), who was sponsor of the Green New Deal bill in the House of Representatives, and the filmmaker Avi Lewis, with animated art by Molly Crabapple and narration by Ocasio-Cortez, it tells the story of the Green New Deal in retrospect, looking back from 2030. After the Democrats won back the White House and Congress in 2020, the film tells us, "We knew that we needed to save the planet, and that we had all the technology to do it."

There is value in the Klein/Crabapple/Ocasio-Cortez/Lewis film and other works that envision a world that we would like to see become reality, along with policies that will be needed to take us there. Such visions can inspire us to act and not be paralyzed by dread and inertia. But it is necessary as well to envision the ways in which our best-laid plans could fail to keep future generations from falling not only into the 2°C world that IPCC projects, but even farther, into the hell of a 3° or 6° world as foreseen by Mark Lynas in his book *Six Degrees* and David Wallace Wells in his book *The Uninhabitable Earth.*[12]

The Earth we knew in the twentieth century is gone, and it's not coming back. The necessity to prevent far more catastrophic heating requires us to impose solid limits that minimize the risk of catastrophe. As we accomplish that, we will have to find a way to live within those limits. New energy technology can be useful in helping us adapt to the limits we impose on ourselves, but it is inadequate to the task of restraining society within the energetic, economic, and ecological boundaries that we are compelled to respect.

There is no time for experimentation. Given the emergency we face, climate policy's highest-priority target must be to drive emissions down to zero in time, without fail. It doesn't matter whether a realistic target is considered to be 1.5°, 2°, or even 2.5°C; all of them will require immediate, steep annual reductions. If the policies we decide to pursue turn out to be inadequate, it will be too late to try something else. By the time failure is apparent, there will be no action, no matter how strong, that can keep warming within acceptable limits. A direct, fool-proof plan is needed, and no such plan yet exists. The Green New Deal is a step in the right direction, but it's only a step. To prevent runaway warming, the Green New Deal must be paired with legal mechanisms that directly drive fossil-fuel use down to zero, and on schedule. Taking that route will at least improve the Earth's chances of avoiding the IPCC's beyond-two-degree future and even more calamitous scenarios.

1

꒦꒤꒦

GROWTH AND LIMITS: 1933–2016

"Every day of continued exponential growth brings the world system closer to the ultimate limits to that growth. A decision to do nothing is a decision to increase the risk of collapse."
—Donella Meadows et al., *The Limits to Growth*, 1972[13]

No nation in history has done what the climate emergency now requires the United States and other nations to do. We must decide collectively that we will refrain, forever, from tapping known, rich reserves of easily available energy. It remains to be seen if we can manage that. We and other nations have faced resource limits many times before, but they were not self-imposed. Now they must be. Can we, collectively, of our own free will, put permanent boundaries around extraction of potent mineral energy from the Earth? That clearly will be the most difficult step in taking on the climate challenge. Should we take that step, we can prepare to deal with the consequences by learning from past episodes in which Americans found themselves hemmed in by forces beyond their control and were forced to deal with limits.

Proponents of ambitious climate initiatives have long been fond of historical allusions. The Manhattan Project, the Apollo Program, the Interstate Highway System, the New Deal, and World War II all have been cited as precedents. For our purposes, we can safely set aside purely technical feats such as the bomb, the moon shot, and the interstates. But the New Deal, the wartime mobilization of the 1940s, and other crucial junctures in the decades that followed, offer insights that can be useful to us in responsibly addressing the climate crisis.

Various Green New Deal visions have been explicit in emulating the 1930s New Deal example of using public policy to put society to work and solve big problems. Those and other strategies for a green makeover of the nation's energy systems and infrastructure often hark back to the lightning-speed buildup of productive forces in the 1940s. But that wartime industrial surge was only half the story. The other half was that for a brief four years, the U.S. civilian economy went into emergency mode, becoming almost the opposite of itself, with carefully planned production and strictly limited but equitable civilian consumption. The postwar economic boom of the 1950s and '60s, surfing on a wave of cheap oil and military spending, created the false impression that limits of all kinds had been suspended. But when the energy crisis landed hard in the 1970s, Americans were shocked back into reality, and the decade came to be defined by limits. Restoring and increasing the flows of both fossil energy and wealth became a central mission of the federal government in the 1980s. Finally, through the climate-aware 1990s and 2000s, the need to reduce and eventually eliminate the use of fossil fuels was dismissed time after time on the grounds that economic growth always takes priority.

The 1930s and '40s saw a desperate need to burst through limits imposed by the economic system. Now, we need desperately to pull the economy back within limits set by the Earth's ecosystems. Whether or not our society—or human civilization—can survive the current emergency intact will depend in large measure on whether we take ecological limits seriously.

"COOPERATIVE CAPITALISM"

Crisis was far too mild a word; *emergency* came closer to capturing most Americans' predicament in the early 1930s. The U.S. unemployment rate had vaulted from 3 percent at the time of the 1929 financial crash to 24 percent during the 1932 presidential campaign. Given those numbers, prospects appeared excellent for Franklin D. Roosevelt, the Democratic Party nominee, as he set out to unseat incumbent Republican Herbert Hoover, whose weak free-market tonics had only worsened the downward spiral.

In a campaign speech at the Commonwealth Club in San Francisco, Roosevelt called for a sharp break from long-standing economic orthodoxy. He had come to the conclusion that in America, growth had not just faltered; it had come to an end. The free-market policies of the nineteenth century, he said, were inadequate to address the human catastrophe they had created. Sounding more like a twenty-first-century steady-state economist than a wealthy politician of the 1930s, he declared, "Our task now is not discovery or exploitation of natural resources, or necessarily producing more goods. It is the soberer, less dramatic business of administering resources and plants already in hand, . . . of distributing wealth and products more equitably, of adapting existing economic organization to the service of the people."[14]

In reality, Roosevelt had no intention of knocking out the pillars of capitalism in such a fashion, and once he took office, his actions were not as radical as he had implied in the San Francisco address. But those actions did include a flood of economic legislation that served as inspiration for today's vision of a Green New Deal. In the Roosevelt administration's first hundred days, Congress passed a breathtaking stack of stimulus initiatives that, among other things, provided $3.3 billion for public works—more than the entire federal budget of three years earlier. This came four years before the publication of John Maynard Keynes's epic *The General Theory of Unemployment, Interest and Money*, the book that showed the world why ending a depression or severe recession requires deep-pocketed government intervention in the economy. In a 1999 article, Patrick Renshaw, then of Sheffield University, discussed how the New Deal was built not on a theoretical foundation like the one laid out by Keynes but rather on the "chaos of improvisation." He wrote, "As it struggled to end mass unemployment, the federal government stumbled on this policy, whereby it was forced to act as compensating agent during an economic downturn, spending public money to fill troughs in the trade cycle in order to stimulate revival."[15]

One of the headline initiatives of those first hundred days was the National Industrial Recovery Act (NIRA) of 1933. Declaring a national emergency, the NIRA created the National Recovery Administration (NRA) and gave it the mission of steering private industry toward prosperity. The Recovery Administration was not a mere dispenser of stimulus funds. Rather, its goal was no less than the planning of the entire industrial economy. It aimed its biggest guns at the cutthroat competition that New Dealers saw as driving down wages and prices and deepening the Depression. The Recovery Administration relaxed antitrust enforcement and worked with private industry, through hundreds of business and trade associations, to develop voluntary "codes of fair practices" that would limit production and set wages and prices. The Recovery Administration also guaranteed the right of workers to unionize, even giving union members a voice in the development of the fair-practice codes. Summing up the Recovery Administration's goals, Ira Katznelson, the author of *Fear Itself: The New Deal and the Origins of Our Time*, wrote that it "sought to refloat capitalism and sustain a balanced private economy." This was to be accomplished through economic planning and "corporatism" aimed at eliminating class conflict and curbing what Roosevelt lieutenant Rexford Tugwell called "the anarchy of the competitive system."[16]

As a grand experiment in industrial planning, the Recovery Administration flopped badly. The Southern Democratic members of Congress who had voted for the underlying legislation turned against the Recovery Administration when they saw that Black workers might have to be paid as much as whites. And the voluntary codes ended up being written and edited largely by the trade associations and powerful corporations, with labor having little say in the matter. It was Katznelson's nicely understated conclusion that "uneven class power made planning for cooperative capitalism difficult."[17] In 1935, the Supreme Court delivered the death blow, declaring the Recovery Act unconstitutional. But 1935 also saw the creation of one of the New Deal's most highly visible recovery programs, the Works Progress Administration (WPA). The WPA pumped enormous stimulus into the economy by hiring more than 8 million unemployed Americans to construct countless public works. Meanwhile, the Recovery Act's failed attempt to foster voluntary reform of private industry was eventually succeeded by toothier regulation under the Fair Labor Standards Act of 1938, which mandated the national minimum wage, the eight-hour workday, overtime pay, and the end of child labor.

KIND OF GREEN

With the climate emergency, the Green New Deal is sharply focused on solving the headline issue of our time. The New Deal had its own, less conspicuous green side, one that sought to resolve the headline environmental problem of its day: the Dust Bowl.

Every state but Vermont and Maine experienced at least one period of severe drought between 1930 and 1936. At times, fine brown dust fell like snow across the eastern half of the country; it had flown all the way from the plowed-up wheat lands of the High Plains two thousand miles to the west. Exposed, desiccated soil was being eroded by the region's characteristic high winds, filling the sky and drifting in roadside ditches. In 1932, there were fourteen major dust storms, each covering vast portions of the region; that annual total rose to sixty-eight in 1936 and seventy-two in 1938. According to the historian Donald Worster, it took a monster record-breaking dust storm in May 1934, to finally "make the plains visible to Washington." He wrote, "As dust sifted down on the Mall and the White House, Roosevelt was in a press conference promising that the Cabinet was at work on a new Great Plains relief program."[18]

In general, the Dust Bowl and the economic devastation of Depression-era rural America sprang from the same roots: The drive for maximum production resulted in maximum exploitation of the soil, at the same time creating a massive glut of grain that an impoverished populace couldn't afford to buy. Worster put in this way:

> Linking the two disasters was a shared cause—a common economic culture, in factories and on farms, based on unregulated private capital seeking its own unlimited increase. In the 1920s that culture had created a high-producing, high-consuming life for Americans. Few people at that time questioned its premises; business was the national faith. But it could also be, as both the bread lines and the dust storms of the following decade revealed, a self-destructive culture, cutting away the ground from under people's feet.[19]

The immediate economic problem was addressed by the Agricultural Adjustment Act (AAA), passed in 1933. Under the act, the Department of Agriculture worked out agreements to reduce production and raise prices to farmers for the major crops and animal products as it sought to get rid of surpluses and expand markets. Later, the Food Stamp Plan was created not only to address widespread hunger, but also to pump up demand for agricultural commodities.[20] The most prominent initiative aiming directly at the Dust Bowl was the Soil Conservation Service (SCS). The agency was created in 1935 by Public Law 74-46, which declared that "the wastage of soil and moisture resources on farm, grazing, and forest lands . . . is a menace to the national welfare."[21] The Soil Conservation Service undertook numerous projects, both in the arid High Plains and also farther east, where rainstorms caused severe "gully erosion." The efforts included acquiring unoccupied land and running public demonstrations of soil-conservation practices such as terrace-building; planting wind-blocking rows of trees with the U.S. Forest Service; subsidizing farmers' soil-saving farming methods; organizing watersheds into Soil Conservation Districts in which farmers were officially designated "cooperators"; and launching many valuable research and extension programs.[22]

Another greenish initiative of the New Deal era was the Civilian Conservation Corps (CCC). With notions of environmentalism as we now know them then still decades in the future, the Conservation Corps grew out of the Progressive-era conservation tradition, focusing on preserving and managing the nation's "natural" lands rather than preventing ecological damage by industry and agriculture. Between 1933 and 1942, some 3 million young men—and only men—took jobs with the Conservation Corps and headed out to train, live, and work in the nation's forests and grasslands. They planted 2 billion trees, built eight hundred state parks, addressed erosion on 40 million acres, built 13,000 hiking trails, and stocked rivers with more than a million fish. They also took up emergency assignments such as firefighting and flood control. (Other accomplishments, such as building 46,000 vehicle bridges, 10,000 small reservoirs, and a million miles of fence, as well as eradicating almost a half-million "predatory animals" were, by current standards, not so green.)[23]

There are obvious echoes of these laws and agencies in the economic justice and stimulus goals of the Green New Deal. Other agencies also were apt precedents. They included the Rural Electrification Administration, the Tennessee Valley Authority, and the Puerto Rico Reconstruction Administration, among others.

THE UPRISING OF 1934

In their study of the two blockbuster recovery bills passed during Roosevelt's first hundred days in office—the Agricultural Adjustment Act for rural America and the National Industrial Recovery Act for industry—Theda Skocpol and Kenneth Finegold see both measures as efforts to create a new system under which "economic functions formerly shaped by market competition would be planned and regulated in the public interest." Had that goal been achieved, they write, the United States would have ended up with business and labor working together congenially under a "centralized system of politically managed corporatist capitalism." But that plan didn't work out. While the Agricultural Act did lead to long-term federal management of the farm economy, things veered off course in industry, which was dominated by corporations much more powerful than the upstart government agencies that were trying to herd them into collective recovery. Furthermore, the National Recovery Administration's leading officials had been drawn from the business world and were more sympathetic to its desire to maximize private profit than to the noncommercial goal of collectively advancing the public interest. In the end, write Skocpol and Finegold, "the dream of harmony between corporate management and industrial labor dissolved into even more bitter conflict."[24]

The "bitter conflict" was an astonishing labor uprising in 1934 that cross-pollinated with the growing social movements of the unemployed, students, African American communities, and farmers, along with local political movements such as the Minnesota Farmer-Labor Party and the Progressive Party in Wisconsin. A general strike in San Francisco spurred long-term militancy up and down the West Coast.

Tens of thousands of unemployed people helped striking workers in Toledo fight off National Guardsmen and scabs. A labor struggle in Minneapolis drew help from the Farmer-Labor Party and a radical group called the Farmers Holiday Association. There was a surge in radical organizing in Detroit's auto industry. The labor uprising and the violent response to it by police, corporate security forces, and the National Guard struck terror in the hearts of national politicians, some of whom started talking publicly about the prospect of open industrial warfare, revolution, and even the imminent opening of the "gates of Hell."[25]

The radical labor upsurge of 1934 was essential to passage of one of the most important pieces of 1930s legislation: the National Labor Relations Act (NLRA), which would guarantee the right of workers to form independent trade unions. The bill had been fiercely opposed by employers, business owners, many members of Congress, and even some on the Left, who saw it as too business-friendly. But with a labor revolt under way nationwide, mainstream leaders came to see the Labor Relations Act as the necessary alternative to permanent industrial turmoil or even Communism. The bill's chief sponsor, Senator Robert Wagner of New York, cited the uprising as a compelling reason to pass the act. The unrest posed a dire threat not only to capitalists but also to the American Federation of Labor (AFL), the mild-mannered organization that had officially been representing organized labor for decades. Its leader, desperate to see the passage of the Labor Relations Act in order to help quell the uprising, went a little radical himself, announcing to a massive rally in Madison Square Garden that if Congress did not pass the act, the AFL would lead a national general strike.[26]

The Labor Relations Act ended up passing easily and was signed into law by Roosevelt. It benefited the working class for decades, but, not surprisingly, the 1934 uprising's aim of reversing the imbalance of power between capital and labor was never achieved. Indeed, in recent decades, the labor movement has lost enough power to take it all the way back to 1932.

Like the Labor Relations Act, ambitious legislation aimed to resolve the climate crisis is likely to pass only if there is a broad-based, grassroots uprising that leaves Congress no option but to pass it. And the Labor Relations Act example suggests that getting laws passed is only the beginning; they have to be backed up by long-term public support demanding that they be enforced in both letter and spirit.

"RAISE PLENTY OF HELL"

The Green New Deal breaks most sharply with its 1930s namesake on one issue in particular: race. Recognizing that the New Deal had the effect of cementing rather than dissolving institutional racism, the drafters of the Green New Deal have kept marginalized communities at the forefront in every document they have turned out so far.

Steve Valocchi of Trinity College in Connecticut was one of many scholars who argued that the New Deal didn't just ignore racial discrimination; in several ways, it directly harmed Black communities. The Works Progress Administration, for example, allowed payment of locally prevailing wages, which hurt people living in predominantly Black areas. Earlier, the National Recovery Administration had similarly allowed lower wages in the South and in occupations that were dominated by Black workers. The underwriting manual of the Federal Housing Administration required banks to, in effect, perpetuate residential segregation:

> Areas surrounding a location are investigated to determine whether incompatible racial and social groups are present, for the purpose of making a prediction regarding the probability of the location being invaded by such groups. If a neighborhood is to retain stability, it is necessary that properties shall continue to be occupied by the same social and racial classes. A change in social or racial occupancy generally contributes to instability and a decline in values.[27]

Finally, there were no significant New Deal initiatives to guarantee civil rights or voting rights or to fight racial discrimination; those would have to wait another thirty years.

Several policies unjustly shortchanged the 40 percent of Black Americans who were working in agriculture at that time. For example, many Black sharecroppers never received payments for which they were eligible, either because the local office of the Adjustment Agency failed to disburse the funds to them, or landowners held the money back on the pretext of covering bills. Some plantation owners who were paid to take their cotton crop out of production would evict the Black tenant farmers who were cultivating that land. Meanwhile, another New Deal headliner, the Social Security Act, did not cover farm laborers or domestic workers, and two-thirds of all Black people employed at the time were working in those occupations.[28]

One of the more courageous and tenacious campaigns of resistance to the New Deal's built-in racial discrimination was launched in 1934 by the Southern Tenant Farmers Union (STFU). Black and white sharecroppers and farmworkers across northeast Arkansas, angered with being cheated by planters and the Agricultural Adjustment Agency, began organizing door-to-door and field-to-field, with encouragement from the Socialist Party and its leader, Norman Thomas. By late 1935, they had formed two hundred local chapters with a total of 25,000 members. In September of that year, five thousand members of the Southern Tenant Farmers Union staged a successful strike for higher wages. That brought a surge of enthusiasm and a flood of new members.[29] In his May 1936 account of the Arkansas rebellion, Jerold Auerbach wrote:

> Union members marched hundreds abreast across the cotton fields to gather additional recruits. Instead, they incensed planters and politicians. Memphis police broke picket lines at the Harahan bridge; striking croppers were arrested and leased to planters to work off their fines and court costs; and a Crittenden County landlord built and filled a small concentration camp. On the fourth day of the strike Governor Futrell sent in National Guardsmen and State Rangers and the union quietly surrendered.[30]

In another incident, cops assaulted and jailed the organizer of a new chapter of the union, a Black minister. A delegation of fifty white sharecroppers with a lawyer in tow managed to get the minister released. But Arkansas landowners, local cops, and the state government were proving to be crueler and more recalcitrant than the local officials from the Adjustment Agency and the New Dealers in Washington.[31]

The union's strategy was to combine "relentless pressure on the New Deal with trade union tactics," but, wrote Auerbach,

> Viewed from the perspective of traditional trade unionism, the organizing drive of the Southern Tenant Farmers Union seemed an anomaly. Its most effective weapons were agitation and publicity, not strikes or collective bargaining. During these early years, the union's organizing drive always had twin objectives: recruitment of new members and propagation of radical alternatives to New Deal agricultural policy. The Southern Tenant Farmers Union sought to organize a protest movement no less than to organize the sharecroppers.[32]

The union newspaper's call to action was, "Raise plenty of Hell and you will get somewhere."[33] The hell-raisers of the Southern Tenant Farmers Union deserve much credit for bringing to America's attention the racial injustices that were built into the New Deal.

THE WAR CURE

Roosevelt worried that if his efforts failed and the Depression dragged on, it would send a message to the world that democracies are ill-equipped to deal with severe economic crises, and this at a time when fascism was on a winning streak in Europe and Japan. Early on, the head of the National Recovery Administration, Hugh Johnson, and other New Dealers had even openly admired the way the dictator Benito Mussolini was handling Italy's economy, but that sort of talk ended in 1935 with the Italian invasion of Ethiopia.[34] Then, in a quick twist of history, it was the 1940s fight against fascism that finally brought full employment and prosperity back to the United States. (Almost eight decades later, the Green New Deal is being envisioned at a time when

Americans are once again confronting a slide toward authoritarianism, if not full-blown fascism—this time not only in Europe and Asia but in Washington, DC, as well.[35])

In 1936, the Roosevelt administration, concluding that the recovery it had jump-started could sustain itself, decided to start easing off the stimulus spigot. Federal spending dropped by 25 percent over two years, and unemployment promptly leaped by a quarter, to 19 percent by 1938. This economic decline was even steeper than that of 1929–33, and unemployment remained above 14 percent until 1941.[36]

Supplying allied nations already at war in Europe while at the same time building up the U.S. arsenal and inducting millions into the military finally accomplished what the New Deal could not. By 1940, Congress had spent $62 billion over eight years trying to dig itself out of the Depression. In the next five years, it would spend $321 billion on World War II—according to Patrick Renshaw, more than the U.S. government had spent *in total* from 1790 to 1940. Heavy spending on the war buildup and consequent massive hiring by both the military and the private sector worked like magic. Over the next four years, the gross national product doubled and the unemployment rate fell to a mere 1.2 percent.[37]

The fact that U.S. industries could ramp up production to a historically unprecedented output within months in support of urgent national goals has inspired present-day visions of a similar industrial mobilization to combat greenhouse warming. There has been less discussion of the deep adaptations that were required of the wartime economy. Overnight, a government that had struggled for a decade with an excess of production and a deficit of consumer buying power had to figure out how to start serving a population that had plenty of money to spend but now faced shortages of goods on which to spend it. The economy had gone from cash-limited to resource-limited. If nothing were done, Depression-era price deflation would flip into just-as-destructive hyperinflation. The federal government responded, tiptoeing into the murky waters of price controls. Under the Office of Price Administration, the process began in 1940 with voluntary campaigns, one commodity at a time, and by 1943 had escalated into a mandatory clampdown on prices throughout the economy.[38]

Enforcing ceilings on prices is a sure, direct way to stop inflation, but it doesn't guarantee fair access. Suppressed prices boost the demand for goods but not the supply. And in the 1940s, supplies of goods were further limited by the diversion of workers and resources into the effort to win the war. The U.S. government was eventually forced into a second level of intervention to make sure that the entire population had access to an adequate supply of food, shelter, clothing, and other basic necessities.

SHRINK, STANDARDIZE, SIMPLIFY

Washington had thrown in the towel in its effort to institute economic planning during the Depression. Now, with a resource-intensive effort to win a war in Asia and Europe, and with the threat of critical shortages at home, planning of production and consumption would become the rule in both the military and civilian economies. A month after the United States entered World War II, a War Production Board (WPB) was created to allocate resources between the military and civilian sectors, ensure an adequate flow of resources to industries supplying crucial civilian goods, and regulate or ban production of other goods.

The degree to which the War Production Board was able to successfully restructure the economy was astonishing. It ordered a halt to all car manufacturing in Detroit and converted the factories for production of tanks and other military vehicles. Non-military sales of mechanical refrigerators were barred in February 1942, and all production was halted in April, saving a quarter-million tons of critical metals over the next year. WPB blocked production of any new air conditioners used "solely for personal comfort" and ordered that air-conditioning systems in some big-city retail stores be removed and installed in far-flung armament factories. Other regulated goods included lumber, bolts, industrial chemicals, bedsprings, farm equipment, cooking stoves, coal- and oil-fired heating stoves, pressure cookers, and even used washing machines.[39]

Authorities sought ways of deeply reducing civilian rail travel to conserve coal. Brewers were restricted in the number of railcars they could use per month for shipping beer, and they were prohibited from hiring trucks to haul additional product. Shipping of retail packages measuring less than sixty inches in length plus girth or weighing under five pounds was prohibited. With ammonia manufacturers feeding the production of explosives for the military, farmers' supplies of nitrogen fertilizer were cut off, and availability of organic fertilizers was limited.

While restricting the production and sale of some products, the War Production Board issued standardized and simplified manufacturing specifications for a whole host of others, explaining that "[s]implification, as it is applied in the war program, is a procedure for eliminating unessentials from an item or a line of items. It reduces the number of items in a line and the variety of style, size, color, or ornamentation not actually necessary to the efficiency or usefulness of the product."[40] The quantity of metal allowed in light fixtures was cut by 60 to 80 percent. A limited range of sizes was specified for glass jars used for preserving vegetables and fruits, and to save metal, glass-top seals and thinner rings were prescribed. The standardization and simplification program covered a wide range of other products, including women's dresses, work uniforms, shoes, socks, stockings, blankets, wooden furniture, and farm machinery parts.[41]

The mandatory channeling of a large share of the nation's resources into the war effort, along with the extensive regulation of civilian production, constricted the supply of some consumer goods. At the same time, price controls kept demand high, raising the specter of shortages, rushes on essential goods, hoarding, and under-the-table selling at high prices to more affluent customers. The nation had gotten its fill of bread lines during the Depression and would tolerate no more of that. But simply lifting price controls would have left lower-income households without adequate access to basic necessities. There remained open only one efficient and just course of action: fair-shares rationing.

In the simpler of the two types of rationing systems, households were issued a monthly set of stamps, each of which specified the physical quantity of a rationed product (e.g., pounds of sugar) that could be purchased. Some classes of goods—most famously, meats, cheese, and butter—were covered by a different system called "points rationing," under which each product in a class was assigned a point "price." For example, for meats, it might mean three points per pound for hamburger and twelve for steak. Ration stamps for these products were denominated in units of points rather than physical quantity.

During 1942–43, a broad range of goods were brought into the rationing system: fuel oil, kerosene, gasoline, tires, cars, bicycles, stoves, typewriters, shoes, coffee, sugar, meats, canned fish, canned milk, cheese, fats, and processed foods. People seemed to complain most about the systems for rationing gasoline and rubber. Those living in Eastern states were even hit with a ban on "pleasure driving." Drivers were told they could obtain additional gasoline for commuting to work, but only after they formed a "car club" with at least three other passengers. For food products, price controls and rationing had some salutary effects, not only prompting families across the country to plant 22 million "victory gardens," but also improving nutrition in all economic classes. Civilian consumption of protein *rose* 11 percent during the rationing period. Increases for calcium and vitamin A were 12 percent, for vitamin C, 8 percent, and for vitamin B1, 41 percent.[42]

Washington moved very cautiously early in the war. War planners imposed price controls and rationing only when they were unavoidable, and made ration limits as generous as possible. The government was perhaps too cautious. In August 1942, when there were only a few products under ration, 70 percent of consumers told pollsters they felt that more extensive rationing was needed in order to eliminate shortages and other problems. Six months later, with controls starting to broaden and tighten, 60 percent of people polled by Gallup still believed that the government should have acted more quickly in rationing scarce goods. Later, when rationing was at its zenith, approval outweighed disapproval by two to one.[43] The wartime experience of the 1940s suggests that rationing is well tolerated or even popular when it is a response to a clearly perceived national crisis.

THE AGE OF LIMITS

In the 1930s and '40s, the U.S. and world economies were far smaller than they are today, and greenhouse emissions were far lower. Earthlings, all but a tiny handful, were blissfully unaware that continuing fossil-fuel-enabled growth would one day become a mortal threat to civilization. The original New Deal was free to aim strictly at restoration of financial stability and prosperity. There were plenty of fuels and raw materials sitting there waiting to be put to work, and the biggest environmental problem, the Dust Bowl, could be fixed in the course of restoring the economy of the Plains.

During the war mobilization that followed, the government spent funds at eight times the rate it had spent fighting the Depression. As far as I know, no one complained at the time about the 65 percent increase in fossil energy consumption that occurred between 1935 and 1945, thanks to the growing economy.[44] Even if there had been prophetic scientists within the growing federal bureaucracy of the 1930s sounding the alarm on future global warming, few, if any, planners would have considered holding back on carbon release before the fight against fascism could be won.

The New Deal legacy, World War II, and a free-flowing bonanza of fossil fuels propelled the postwar U.S. economy into a long, high-glide trajectory. But they also masked an underlying drag on economic growth, according to a landmark book by Paul Baran and Paul Sweezy, *Monopoly Capital*,[45] published in 1966. The two Marxian economists saw the United States becoming increasingly dominated by shrinking numbers of giant corporations, thereby developing a long-term tendency toward stagnation. A decade in the writing, the book applied and extended Marx's analysis of capitalism to this mid-twentieth-century phenomenon, one that Baran and Sweezy dubbed "monopoly capital."

The New Dealers had weakened antitrust regulation, and the concentration of economic power had continued to deepen during and after World War II. *Monopoly Capital*'s central idea was that in the postwar period, companies and conglomerates had become so large that they were able to transcend the meat grinder of competition. But in doing so, they were undermining the very engine of economic growth. In such oligopolies, Baran and Sweezy argue, big corporations can set prices with little concern for what their competitors charge, thereby avoiding destructive "price wars." The big firms can also afford the kinds of technologies that allow economic output per worker—productivity—to rise faster than wages. Largely immune to competitive forces and able to churn out more of their products with a smaller payroll while charging higher prices, corporations accumulate vast surpluses of wealth that far exceed the amount that can be absorbed through investment in new capital. The force behind the growth of capitalist economies—the cycle of production, sales, wealth accumulation, reinvestment, and expanded production—gets bogged down, and stagnation results.[46]

In a world dominated by monopoly capital, therefore, economists no longer need inquire into the causes of stagnations or depressions; the question, rather, is how do mature capitalist economies manage to grow at all? After all, *Monopoly Capital*'s argument that there exists a long-term tendency toward stagnation was published twenty years into an unprecedented economic boom. How to explain that? Noting that opportunities for absorbing excess surplus still existed, but that powerful ones were exceedingly rare, Baran and Sweezy point to a small handful of phenomena that had created major capital-investment incentives. Most obviously, there was the war economy, which had ended the stagnation of the 1930s and, thanks to the Cold War and U.S. militarism around the globe, was still pumping adrenaline into the economy of the 1960s. Then there were the massive economies surrounding the private automobile: its manufacture and care, and the related industries that were directly enriched from it, including gasoline, insurance, and tourism. In addition to these were what Baran and Sweezy call the "sales effort," an entire meta-economy led by the advertising and public relations industries. They warned that although these financial engines were capable of driving the U.S. economy further, they all had their own limits. Furthermore, the business cycles inherent in all capitalist economies ensured that growth would never be constant and linear. (Later, from the 1980s onward, militarism, the vehicle industry, hyper-commercialism, and mass advertising would prove to be insufficient forces for boosting mass consumption sufficiently to keep up with ballooning surplus production, so a fourth economic adjustment mechanism, the seemingly limitless growth of financial markets, emerged. The "financialization" wave, as well as those older investment mechanisms, has remained in play and, crucially, together they continue to be some of the dominant contributors to greenhouse warming.

Now the nascent renewable-energy industry is being billed as yet another means of keeping economic stagnation at bay.)

By 1972, gross national product was still growing nicely, and the United States was looking forward to the end of yet another foreign war. At that year's Republican Convention, President Richard Nixon crowed that Americans had "more prosperity than any people in the world, [and] we have the highest rate of growth of any industrial nation."[47] A month later, the *New York Times* reported on forecasts of "continued strong general economic growth" through 1973.[48]

The last thing politicians, economists, or investors wanted to hear about in 1972 was any talk of hindrance, caution, or restraint. So the publication that year of a book titled *The Limits to Growth*[49] was about as welcome as a bowl of prune soup at a potluck. Through the remainder of the twentieth century, the book was widely loathed and dismissed in economic, political, and scientific circles; in this century, with climate chaos making its arguments appear more and more on target, it has gained wide respect.[50]

The Limits to Growth had its roots in a 1968 meeting of what came to be known as the Club of Rome, an international collection of, in their own characterization, "scientists, educators, economists, humanists, industrialists, and national and international civil servants"; the group took its name from the city where that meeting took place. Their broad concern was, as they saw it, the global complex of economic, political, social, cultural, and environment problems.

In the gender-hindered language of the times, Club members later decided to pursue what they called a "Project on the Predicament of Mankind." Their analysis employed then-state-of-the-art computer models developed at the Massachusetts Institute of Technology. The models predicted the trajectories of humanity's and the Earth's vital signs all the way through the twenty-first century, based on several alternative strategies aimed at relieving or circumventing ecological limits and thereby avoiding economic decline or even the collapse of civilization. But every model they tested led to a dangerous "overshoot" of environmental limits. Sometimes it was because of pollution, sometimes resource scarcity, sometimes decline of food production. Any of these, the model predicted, would cut off economic growth sometime before

2100, triggering an irreversible decline. Regarding technology, for example, the book's authors came to a grim conclusion: "When we introduce technological developments that successfully lift some restraint to growth or avoid some collapse, the system simply grows to another limit, temporarily surpasses it, and falls back."

Even in a model that assumed "unlimited" resources, strong pollution controls, increased agricultural productivity, and "perfect" availability and application of family planning, while using every tool at hand "to circumvent in some way the various limits to growth," the result was still an end of growth, caused by three "simultaneous crises:" soil degradation, resource depletion "by a prosperous world population," and dramatic increases in contaminants—among which the modelers presciently included excess atmospheric CO_2 (carbon dioxide.) They concluded that the "application of technological solutions alone has prolonged the period of population and industrial growth, but it has not removed the ultimate limits to that growth."[51]

Finally, they radically altered the model's parameters to portray a society that chooses restraint. For example, they assumed universal access to fully effective birth control and a desired reproduction rate of two children; limits on production; dramatically increased efficiency of resource use and pollution prevention; emphasis on soil protection and universal food security; and better durability of goods and capital stock. That scenario produced not collapse but a world that ended up in an economically modest equilibrium that was adequate to satisfy human needs.

The Limits to Growth was full of graphs depicting future rises and declines of population, resource use, agricultural and industrial production, and pollution, and included a stark warning: "We . . . believe that if a profound correction is not made soon, a crash of some sort is certain. And it will occur within the lifetimes of many who are alive today." For years, the book's critics enjoyed pointing out that the collapses forecasted in the business-as-usual curves had not occurred. Finally, in the early 2000s, a few analysts decided to compare *The Limits to Growth*'s predictions with what had actually happened so far.[52] They found that the world's vital signs had followed the old model's predictions quite closely up to that time. The bad news for us, they pointed out, is that if you follow those ascending business-as-usual curves to which the world is still adhering out to the year 2030, they show industrial and food production peaking out and then collapsing.

THAT SEVENTIES CLAUSTROPHOBIA

Almost exactly a year after publication of *The Limits to Growth*, people in the United States found themselves in their first encounter with general scarcity since World War II. It wasn't the beginning of the collapse portrayed in the book's graphs, but it was a pretty good preview.

In October 1973, an already alarming blast of inflation triggered largely by the prolonged U.S. war in Indochina was exacerbated when Arab nations belonging to the Organization of Petroleum Exporting Countries (OPEC) imposed an oil embargo on Western countries. World oil prices leaped suddenly and dramatically, and gasoline prices in the United States spiraled to unheard-of heights. As inflation impacted the economy, it was perversely accompanied by recession, bringing a new word into the American lexicon: *stagflation*. President Nixon ordered that a World War II-style national allocation plan be put in place to ensure that every region had access to adequate fuel supplies. Once again, pleasure driving was discouraged. Nixon also announced cuts in deliveries of heating oil: 15 percent for homes, 25 percent for businesses, and 10 percent for manufacturers. Aviation fuel was cut 15 percent, and on the nation's highways, the maximum speed limit was lowered to 55 miles per hour.[53]

Long lines at gas stations became an enduring symbol of the 1970s. A more alarming development, one illustrating the severe backlash that governments can face when they attempt to deal with resource limits, was the violent strike by independent truckers that first broke out in December 1973. To back their demands for reduced diesel fuel prices, abolition of the 55 mph speed limit, and general deregulation, the truckers not only stopped hauling but also tried to keep all trucks off the road. Many parked their semis in the middle of highways, while others resorted to throwing bricks, puncturing tires, and brandishing firearms. After the first two rounds of protests, one trucker told the press, "When the next shutdown comes around . . . I'm gonna take my goddamn truck and burn it on the goddamn White House lawn."[54]

The end of the OPEC embargo in 1974 brought just enough relief from gasoline shortages to calm nerves and shorten gas lines, but what would become known as the "energy crisis" was far from over. Upon taking office following Nixon's resignation, President Gerald Ford laid out a plan to reduce the country's dependence on imported oil through taxes and tariffs, but it turned out to be a political disaster for him. And stagflation raged on. President Ford was among those who saw inflation becoming an even greater national threat than unemployment. At one point, he noted that unemployment was "the biggest concern of the 8.2 percent of American workers temporarily out of work," but inflation was "the universal enemy of 100 percent of the people."[55] Any attempt at New Deal–style stimulus to address the stagnation problem would have triggered even worse inflation. Nor was military spending a solution; after all, it was a big part of what had gotten America into its inflationary predicament in the first place.

The oil crisis calmed for a while. But in 1979, the Iranian Revolution sent petroleum prices skyward again. In Levittown, Pennsylvania, a crowd of 1,500 gas rioters reportedly burned cars, destroyed gas pumps, and threw rocks and bottles at police. One officer responded to a question from a motorist by smashing his windshield, whacking the driver's son with his club, and putting the man's wife in a choke hold. In all, eighty-two people were injured, and almost two hundred were arrested. The U.S. media solemnly discussed the possibility of "civilizational breakdown."[56] That summer, inflated diesel prices triggered a revival of the independent truckers' strike. The historian Shane Hamilton described chaos that exceeded that of the 1973–74 strike:

> On June 5, 1979, a convoy of truckers arrived in Washington and circled the Capitol. [Strike leader] Mike Parkhurst seized the moment and called for a nationwide shutdown, not simply to demand lower fuel prices, but to abolish the Interstate Commerce Commission and open up regulated freight trucking to untrammeled competition. By the end of

June, approximately seventy-five thousand truckers heeded Parkhurst's call and stopped driving. Once again the protests were violent, as roving bands of truckers set fire to empty trucks and shot at the windshields of drivers who refused to stop. Nine states called out the National Guard. By the time the shutdown ended in early July, one driver had been shot and killed, dozens more injured.[57]

As enraged truckers were laying siege to Washington, President Carter, by then in his third year in office, prepared to deliver what was being billed as his most important speech yet. It would be his fifth address to the nation on energy policy, a sign of how that issue had so far dominated his presidency. (Four months later, the Iran hostage crisis would displace the energy crisis as his administration's most pressing concern.)

On July 15, 1979, Carter delivered his speech live on prime-time TV.[58] Right at the top, he declared that the threat everyone was calling an energy crisis was actually a crisis of confidence, of self-indulgence, of consumption. "Human identity," he said, "is no longer defined by what one does but what one owns." In an echo of today, he decried the "fragmentation and self-interest" that was roiling the nation. ABC's Frank Reynolds would later characterize that portion of the speech as "almost a sermon." To today's ears, the proposals Carter rolled out in his speech sounded something like a Green New Deal, 1970s-style. He envisioned investing massively in alternative energy sources, restricting oil imports, creating an "Energy Mobilization Board," establishing a "bold conservation program," and making energy affordable to low-income Americans. He proposed spending an additional $10 billion on public transportation and asked Americans "to take no unnecessary trips, to use carpools or public transportation whenever you can, to park your car one extra day per week, to obey the speed limit, and to set your thermostats to save fuel." He added, "Every act of energy conservation like this is more than just common sense, I tell you it is an act of patriotism."[59]

In 1979, the terms Carter used in naming his proposals didn't mean quite what they might during today's climate emergency. The

Energy Mobilization Board's (EMB) mission, for example, would expedite the regulatory process to put high-priority fossil-energy projects on the "fast track." The top tier of projects for the EMB included oil and gas drilling on federal land, extracting oil from shale, coal gasification, coal liquefaction, and building new oil pipelines. Renewable energy and energy conservation projects would be treated as lower-priority initiatives. Less than two weeks after Carter pitched the EMB in his big energy speech, the House voted it down. Concerns, according to one observer, included perceived encroachment upon states' rights, expansion of bureaucracy, and "reluctance by members of the Republican party to support a key element in the President's energy program in an election year."[60]

In his July 15 speech, Carter had also called on Congress to authorize one major energy conservation initiative: a standby plan for rationing gasoline.[61] Although it took a while, Congress passed such a measure in 1980. Five billion ration coupons had been printed up during the Nixon years and were ready to go.[62] Rationing would be triggered in the event of a 20 percent shortfall in the national gasoline supply, and household gasoline allowances would be fixed at 20 percent below normal consumption.[63]

In the end, rationing would not be needed. Oil supplies stabilized, economic stagnation suppressed fuel demand, and the resulting glut pushed world prices down. No future need for rationing was anticipated. Furthermore, the Army reportedly was concerned that if the coupons, which featured an image of George Washington, got out into circulation, change machines might mistake them for dollar bills. In June 1984, Nixon's old coupons were pulled out of storage at the Pueblo Army Depot in Colorado, shredded, and buried.[64]

The energy claustrophobia of the 1970s was summed up by historian Jefferson Cowie:

> [T]he nation running out of energy was both a reality and a metaphor, and the problem of limits shaped the entire discussion. It haunted Richard Nixon, stymied Gerald Ford, all but destroyed the Carter presidency, and opened up the space for the Reagan restoration of the new Gilded Age. . . . By the

time Ford filled in after Nixon's resignation, the litany of a restricted future had become less abstract and more particular
until Carter was forced to concede that "dealing with limits"
was the "subliminal theme" of his presidency.[65]

Carter had declared in his 1979 speech that "beginning this moment, this nation will never use more foreign oil than we did in 1977—
never." But the president did not reaffirm that pledge in his 1980 State
of the Union address. Instead, in response to the Soviet invasion of
Afghanistan two months before, he announced what came to be known
as the Carter Doctrine. The United States would put the world on notice that it would use military force to protect its interests in Southwest
Asia, the Arabian Peninsula, and other oil-rich regions.

After almost four subsequent decades of burning fossil fuels—and
having seen the beginnings of the climatic impact of all those emissions—we can ask whether the energy conservation proposals of the
1970s could have evolved into a transition to independence from fossil
fuels. To take one small example, if Congress's standby gas-rationing
plan had been triggered, and had per-capita consumption remained at
the rationed amount until the present day (taking population increase
into account), we could have saved 920 billion gallons, more than six
years of today's U.S. gasoline consumption.[66] That would have kept
9 billion tons of CO_2 out of the atmosphere. It wouldn't have been
enough to prevent the climate emergency, but perhaps forty years of
living under such a limit could have set off a chain reaction of progressive moves throughout the economy aimed at dealing with energetic
and ecological limits. Left unconstrained, however, the fossil fuel business, and the myriad commercial goods and services that extend from
on it, continued to grow like unchecked tumors.

One legacy of the 1970s did persist: the Carter Doctrine. Ensuring
the flow of fossil energy became a top priority for the U.S. military,
which, not coincidentally, has become one of the world's largest petroleum consumers. Several wars later, much of our armed presence
around the world remains dedicated to securing U.S. access to foreign
oil, natural gas, and other mineral resources.

MAKING FOSSIL AMERICA GREAT AGAIN—AGAIN

Federal energy and environmental policy would suffer a severe case of whiplash following the inauguration of President Ronald Reagan in 1981. Toward the end of Reagan's first term, James Everett Katz of the University of Texas wrote that the president had "returned the USA to an era when the energy industry and the government cooperated amiably with each other. Gone are the equity concerns that were an integral part of the Nixon, Ford and Carter Administrations' energy policies. Instead, a minimum of governmental involvement in energy planning is advocated, and Reagan's energy philosophy has backed free market forces instead."[67]

Six months into that first term, Reagan's team put out a National Energy Plan, which turned out to be a search-and-destroy mission against any of the even faintly green or humanitarian provisions that had been in previous energy plans under Carter.[68] All conservation and renewable energy policies were targeted for elimination. Consideration of social impacts? Gone. Price controls to keep fuel and utility bills within reach of low-income households? Out. Consumer protection? Sorry, no more of that. Katz noted, "The plan also offers little hope that the government will take an active role in handling energy shortages or emergencies."

Decontrol of oil prices meant a profit windfall for oil corporations and a tax windfall for the government, because higher prices did not reduce consumption. In 1981, the number of leases for offshore oil and gas drilling reached double the previous year's number. Congress passed a $12 billion tax cut for individuals and investors who had income derived from oil. Meanwhile, the budget for solar energy was cut to the bone, and funds for energy conservation dropped from $780 million to $190 million in three years. "To the Reagan Administration," wrote Katz, "emphasis on conservation implies personal sacrifice, limits on future economic growth, and a dismal future for the USA and capitalism." Reagan's energy plan departed from free-market doctrine in only one sector: He urged vigorous government support for the fiscally ailing, uninsurable nuclear power industry.[69]

At the 1980 Republican National Convention, Reagan had promised, "For those who've abandoned hope, we'll welcome them into a great national crusade to make America great again." But like the candidate who would appropriate that slogan thirty-five years later, Reagan would do a lot more for the fossil fuel industry than for "those who've abandoned hope." Katz concluded that Reagan and the Republicans showed "indifference to values most of the country has adopted since the Great Depression 50 years ago," while their energy policy was "heavily weighted against Administration opponents (liberal Democrats, environmentalists and conservationists) and in favor of supporters (Western and Sunbelt energy producers and their representatives in Congress, and the nuclear industry)."[70] In energy policy as in other ways, the United States of 2017 would reverberate with echoes of 1981.

The 1970s and '80s sent us an unmistakable message: We can always count upon Republican administrations to support maximum fossil-fuel and nuclear energy, whatever ecological destruction results, and we cannot count on Democratic administrations to resolve energy or ecological crises if they aren't being pushed to do it by a grassroots rebellion. Now the twenty-first century is sending the same message.

TICK-TOCK GOES THE CLIMATE CLOCK

In the year 1700, the concentration of CO_2 in the Earth's atmosphere was about 270 parts per million (ppm). By 1980, after a quarter millennium of burning fossil fuels, it had reached 339 ppm, but few were paying attention. The world did start worrying by 1988, however, when the Intergovernmental Panel on Climate Change (IPCC) was established to study the situation. By that year, the CO_2 concentration had reached 350 ppm—a figure that two decades later would come to be widely accepted as the limit beyond which, in the words of superstar climate scientist James Hansen and colleagues, maintaining a world "similar to the one on which civilization developed and to which life on earth is adapted" would eventually become impossible.[71]

Over the next thirty years, scientists, governments, international bodies, think tanks, and climate-action groups set off louder and louder alarms about the torrent of greenhouse gases inundating the Earth's atmosphere. Countless conferences would debate arcane policies and even produce international agreements. But all such efforts were stymied by a consensus for inaction among the United States and other governments. They feared that if the world were to take effective action on greenhouse emissions, economic growth would be hampered. As the years rolled on, the accumulation of wealth proceeded on schedule with just a few interruptions, while greenhouse gases continued to accumulate in the sky above.

In 1992, at the Earth Summit in Rio de Janeiro, the UN Framework Convention on Climate Change (UNFCCC) was agreed upon. At the summit, President George H.W. Bush claimed for his country the right to sustain growth, whatever the impact on the Earth, by infamously declaring, "The American way of life is not up for negotiation."[72] That year, the U.S. GDP stood at $6.5 trillion, and atmospheric CO_2 had risen to 356 ppm.[73]

In 1997, the Kyoto Protocol, a global emissions-cutting treaty, was adopted. President Bill Clinton signed it. Vice President Al Gore, who would go on to become a leading climate advocate, was in attendance and insisted that "any reductions [of greenhouse emissions] be implemented through the market-based trading of 'rights to pollute.'" Later, the U.S. Senate refused to ratify Kyoto, with Idaho Senator Larry Craig declaring that Clinton's signing of the treaty was "the first time in history that an American president has allowed foreign interests to control and limit the growth of the U.S. economy."[74] GDP was $8.6 trillion. CO_2 stood at 363 ppm.

In 2001, newly elected President George W. Bush erased Clinton's Kyoto signature, claiming that the treaty "would have wrecked our economy."[75] GDP was at $10.6 trillion and CO_2 at 370 ppm.

In 2008, United Nations officials and economists proposed a Green New Deal to pull the world economy out of the incipient Great Recession. The UN Environment Program's executive director declared, "The new, green economy would provide a new engine of growth, putting the world on the road to prosperity again."[76] U.S. GDP was $14.7 trillion, and CO_2 was up to 385 ppm.

In 2015, the Obama Administration's climate negotiators, fearful of constraining the economy, significantly weakened the Paris Agreement on climate. They successfully demanded that a single word in the document be changed, so that the United States and other developed countries would agree that they "should" rather than "shall" undertake economy-wide quantified emission reductions.[77] GDP had reached $18.2 trillion, while CO_2 had risen to within one-half part per million of 400.

In 2017, President Donald Trump withdrew U.S. support from the Paris Agreement, saying, "This agreement is less about the climate and more about other countries gaining a financial advantage over the United States." He used the word "climate" only twice more in his statement, both times dismissively, while using the word "economy" or "economic" nineteen times.[78] GDP stood at 19.5 trillion, CO_2 at 405 ppm.

For a quarter century, the rise in atmospheric CO_2 concentration was left unrestrained thanks to the single-minded focus of Big Business and its backers in governments worldwide on limitless economic growth. The toothless Paris Agreement would not have broken that stalemate, but the election of Trump and the demise of Paris did set off alarms across the globe. The United States would be stuck with national climate inaction, and worse, for a few years; by the time action would again be possible, we'd be playing a game of catch-up, and nothing short of a big, far-reaching mobilization would have any chance of succeeding.

2

≈⊰⊱≈

"WHAT THE HELL HAPPENED?": 2016–2020

"We children are doing this for you to put your differences aside and start acting as you would in a crisis. We children are doing this because we want our hopes and dreams back.

I hope my microphone was on. I hope you could all hear me."

—climate activist Greta Thunberg, addressing the
UK Parliament, April 23, 2019

Like many Americans, Margaret Klein Salamon remembers well what went through her mind the moment she awoke on the morning of November 9, 2016. "I think I wanted to die," she recalls. "Those were some of the darkest times of my adult life. I was feeling horrible, like most of the people in my network were, but I was feeling extra horrible because all of our planning, everything we had been working for, had been washed away."[79]

On that morning after the election of Donald J. Trump to the presidency of the United States, says Ezra Silk, "I felt like the whole world had just flipped upside down. I was convinced we were on the verge of collapse. And I might not have been wrong. I might just have been early! But it quickly became obvious to me that the organizing and power-building required to actually pull off a climate mobilization will have to be massive."[80]

Salamon and Silk are co-founders of The Climate Mobilization, a group that has developed a detailed road map for doing just that:

mobilizing society to address an ecological emergency that is not looming in some far-off time, but unfolding before our eyes in the present.[81] For them and many other climate activists, the first ten months of 2016 had been full of hope that an incoming Democratic president and Congress would tackle the climate emergency with vigor. Now, with the White House and both houses of Congress controlled by far-right forces hostile to any form of climate action, the despair felt by Salamon and Silk on that November 9 morning was shared by millions of Americans who understood that Washington would be dominated by climate deniers for several years to come.

The worst fears were realized when, almost immediately after Inauguration Day, President Trump and the entire executive branch began taking actions that seemed designed to encourage *increased* emissions of greenhouse gases and other pollutants, along with further degradation of the nation's soils, waters, and ecosystems. Federal agencies began removing the term "climate change" from documents and even deleting entire climate-related documents—sometimes on the orders of Trump political appointees and other times as a defensive move, out of fear of attack from the White House. This Orwellian editing had real-world consequences; for example, EPA's move to take down a website describing the Obama-era Clean Power Plan facilitated the eventual gutting of the plan.[82] These and other attacks on the environment helped spark a surge in climate activism, a surge that would build through the years to come.

The climate crisis, historically ignored by politicians seeking office, became one of the top issues in the election campaigns of 2018 and 2019–20. A year before the 2020 Democratic primaries, the climate crisis polled as a top issue, along with health care, among primary voters.[83] And the center of gravity in the discussion to solve the climate emergency became a broad set of visionary proposals known as the Green New Deal.

The Green New Deal appeared to come roaring in out of nowhere to attract far more attention and debate than any previous climate initiative. Various proposals going by that name had been simmering in Europe and the United States for a decade, but now a shift in public consciousness that cleared a wide path to the center of political life for this version of the Green New Deal. That shift seemed to happen suddenly, but the energy behind it had started building well before November 2016, in places far removed from Washington, D.C.

SHOWDOWN ON THE MISSOURI

On Earth Day, April 22, 2016, the United States, along with most of the world's other nations, signed the Paris Agreement to reduce greenhouse emissions. The grassroots climate movement responded with only tepid applause. The pact had been significantly watered down at the insistence of the United States and other rich-world nations. In announcing the signing, even President Obama acknowledged its shortcomings, saying, "Now, the Paris Agreement alone will not solve the climate crisis. Even if we meet every target embodied in the agreement, we'll only get to part of where we need to go."[84]

Climate activists eager to leapfrog Paris and aim for bolder climate goals saw that year's presidential election campaign as an opportunity. On July 9, 2016, members of the Democratic Platform Committee were assembled in a hotel conference room in Orlando, Florida, working on the climate-and-environment plank, when supporters of Bernie Sanders moved to insert language calling for a World War II–style climate mobilization to marshal a "green industrial revolution." The text read:

> Democrats believe it would be a grave mistake for the United States to wait for another nation to lead the world in combating the global climate emergency. In fact, we must move first in launching a green industrial revolution, because that is the key to getting others to follow; and because it is in our own national interest to do so. Just as America's greatest generation led the effort to defeat the Axis Powers during World War II, so must our generation now lead a World War II–type national mobilization to save civilization from catastrophic consequences. We must think beyond Paris. In the first 100 days of the next administration, the President will convene a summit

of the world's best engineers, climate scientists, climate experts, policy experts, activists and indigenous communities to chart a course toward the healthy future we all want for our families and communities.[85]

The motion to include the text had been made by California delegate Russell Greene. Rising in support, David Braun, also from California, argued for the ambitious vision, telling fellow delegates that the Democratic Party was uniquely suited to mobilize the nation, because, he reminded them, "we are the party of the New Deal!" The motion passed with almost no opposition. Although there is much in any party platform that never becomes reality, the delegates' strong support for climate mobilization, for getting beyond Paris, created a sense of possibility.

Meanwhile, 2,000 miles northwest of Orlando, a grassroots mobilization was already well under way. For years, much on-the-ground climate action had targeted the petroleum industry, chiefly over extraction methods—hydraulic fracturing in gas fields, strip mining in tar sands—along with the construction of long-distance oil pipelines, most prominently the Keystone XL. In the fall of 2016, as election season heated up, so did an extraordinary standoff along the Missouri River in North Dakota, on the Standing Rock Reservation. That April, a handful of young Native Americans had set up camp near a spot where the innocuously named company Energy Transfer Partners was planning to extend a pipeline leading from the Dakota oil fields up to and under the bed of the Missouri River, to eventually connect to depots in Illinois. The Dakota Access Pipeline would cut a huge gash through the reservation, violate ecosystems and sacred Indigenous sites, threaten the reservation's water supply, and help streamline the extraction and burning of fossil fuels.

Through the summer, the population of the encampment grew from hundreds to thousands of people, and came to include members of hundreds of tribes, as well as many non-Native activists. Kelly Hayes, a Native organizer and nonviolent direct-action trainer, took part in the protests. She later wrote,

For Native people, the camps marked a cultural intersection between prayer and protest. The term Water Protector emerged as a descriptor for those holding space to stop the pipeline. It was a time of spectacular convergence. Centuries-old feuds between Native peoples were put aside, as once-hostile tribes joined the camps, bearing tobacco, firewood, and other gifts. The space was full of songs, history, and potential. From quiet, prayerful marches to complex lockdowns that halted construction equipment, a new chapter of our history was being written, in real time. For Native people, 2016 was a year of tension, hope, and action.[86]

As the spontaneous, nonviolent community at Standing Rock grew, it was met with escalating state violence. In September and October, while the rest of the country remained transfixed by an increasingly rancorous election campaign, the camps came under all-out assault. Police, state troopers, the National Guard, and private security forces, aiming to clear the way for the pipeline, deployed a nasty array of weaponry: batons, pepper spray, dogs, tear gas, rubber bullets, water cannons, "long-range acoustic devices" (a.k.a. "sound cannons"), concussion grenades, and armored assault vehicles.

Despite the attacks, the camps remained in place into the frigid Dakota winter and even chalked up a win on December 4, when the outgoing Obama administration denied Energy Transfer Partners a permit to run the pipeline under the river. By then, however, not only Standing Rock but the broader climate/justice community were bracing for the Category 5 political storm that would strike Washington on January 20, 2017, with Trump's inauguration. As expected, on just his second full working day in office, Trump signed executive orders clearing the way for both the Dakota Access Pipeline and the Keystone XL Pipeline.

THE SEARCH FOR A WORKAROUND

Three weeks after Trump was elected, in an essay for Portland Rising Tide, Arnold Shroder noted that the opening for building a bigger, more radical, more effective movement may have actually widened. People in the United States could no longer sit back and wait for Washington to take action; therefore, he wrote, "Federal intransigence on climate is such that most plausible scenarios for significant near-term emissions reductions involve states, counties, and municipalities . . . to find diverse and creative ways to dismantle their fair share of the fossil fuel economy." However, most local and state officials were still going to act only when pushed to do so, meaning that intense public pressure and bold approaches would be needed. "Direct action," Shroder continued, "can influence the behavior of political entities which are capable of significantly impeding Trump's agenda."[87]

State and local governments did push back. That summer, a month after Trump announced that he would withdraw the United States from the Paris Agreement, California governor Jerry Brown and former New York City mayor Michael Bloomberg launched America's Pledge, a project to document and promote the efforts of states and cities to reduce their greenhouse emissions at the Paris-prescribed rate. Two national networks were involved in those efforts: the U.S. Climate Alliance of fourteen states and Puerto Rico, comprising 36 percent of the U.S. population and 40 percent of the country's GDP; and U.S. Climate Mayors, representing 383 cities that were home to almost one-fourth of the national population. Policies varied broadly from state to state and city to city, but America's Pledge compiled a list of more than fifty specific initiatives that had already been undertaken, ranging from non-fossil energy goals to incentives for energy-efficient vehicles to food-waste reduction to bike-sharing programs. It was difficult to quantify the potential of the diverse assortment of initiatives to reduce greenhouse emissions, and America's Pledge admitted that state and local governments would be unable to compensate fully for federal hostility toward climate action, even if they aimed only for the wholly inadequate Paris targets: "Given the stated policies of the present U.S. administration, currently committed non-federal efforts are not sufficient to meet the U.S. commitment under the Paris Agreement to reduce emissions 26–28 percent below 2005 levels."[88]

One of the most comprehensive local efforts emerged in Los Angeles. In October, The Climate Mobilization, along with L.A.

city councilmember Paul Koretz, kicked off an initiative called Climate Justice Mobilization 2025, with the mission of achieving a carbon-neutral Los Angeles within eight years. The means to that end would be not just the usual buffet of assorted green initiatives but rather a "World War II-scale climate mobilization rooted in environmental justice."[89] More than a thousand local governments around the world would eventually issue climate emergency declarations, committing to a "rapid, just transition away from fossil fuels."

The Green New Deal was not to be the first climate-related bill introduced on Capitol Hill in the Trump era. In the politically inclement spring of 2017, Senators Jeff Merkley (D-Ore.) and Bernie Sanders (D-Vt.) co-sponsored a climate bill known as the "100 by '50 Act."[90] Writing for the climate group 350.org, Merkley called the bill, S.987, the "most ambitious piece of climate legislation Congress has ever seen."[91] While it did clear that decidedly low bar, the bill's leisurely timetable and lack of a robust mechanism for eliminating fossil fuels from the economy rendered it inadequate to stave off a climate meltdown.

The 100 by '50 Act appeared to have been meant as a compromise banner around which liberals and moderates could rally through those dark times, and then to serve as a launching pad for action, when action became possible down the road. But with no prospect of getting through either chamber of Congress until what then seemed like a far distant future, the bill got very little traction. Then, just as the 100 by '50 Act was fading from memory, America was about to get a lesson in what a disrupted-climate future might look like. Hurricane season had arrived.

PUERTO RICO'S GREEN NEW ORDEAL

The Green New Deal would aim almost exclusively at domestic policy. That makes sense both logically and politically: logically because the U.S. government, having no plan for effective climate action, would have no standing to lecture other nations about greenhouse emissions; and politically because the domestic focus would appeal to Americans' sense of patriotism. Stressing the latter, *Washington Post* columnist Eugene Robinson wrote, perhaps overoptimistically, "Do you really want Beijing to lead the way into the future? Shouldn't it be Washington? That's a rationale for the Green New Deal that the Make America Great Again crowd should embrace. If you believe in American exceptionalism, you believe that the United States has a duty to lead at moments of crisis. This is such a moment."[92]

The emphasis on domestic policies, however, left our climate debt unaddressed.[93] Impoverished countries and marginalized communities around the globe are suffering the consequences of 400-plus ppm CO_2 in the atmosphere, the bulk of it sent there by people in North America and Europe. That our moral obligation to settle the climate debt stretches beyond the borders of our fifty states has typically been denied or ignored by the federal government, but eight months into the Trump presidency and a year before the Green New Deal blasted off, the climate debt suddenly became impossible to ignore. When, in the wake of Hurricane Maria,[94] 3,000 to 4,000 people—possibly more—died and Puerto Rico was left physically devastated and economically crippled, no one could claim that this humanitarian tragedy was some other government's problem.

Puerto Rico, having survived centuries of colonialism, fits the profile of many places around the world that have been rendered highly vulnerable to climate disasters. The people of the island earn only one-third of the median household income of people in the mainland United States, and produce only 37 percent of the of the mainland's per-capita carbon emissions.[95] With Puerto Rico, as with New Orleans's Lower Ninth Ward twelve years earlier, an unnatural disaster struck economically disadvantaged communities of color on U.S. soil.

Despite our country's obvious obligation to put even more resources into Puerto Rico's disaster recovery than we normally do when disasters strike privileged U.S. communities (or maybe because that obligation was too obvious), the Trump administration expended minimal effort and made sure that even the inadequate funds provided to Puerto Rico by Congress were spent to little effect.[96] President Trump reportedly became personally obsessed with punishing the people of the island.[97] But his extreme bigotry and cruelty toward Puerto Ricans should not blind us to the fact that mistreatment is nothing new to Puerto Ricans: Their plight is the result of centuries of colonial domination, the most recent 122 years of which has been dictated by the United States.[98] Maria exacerbated their burden, and the lack of adequate recovery assistance from the federal government tightened the screws several more turns.

Puerto Rico has lost 8 percent of its population since 2015.[99] However, some communities have lost a much larger share of their residents than others. Homes in the Sierra Brava neighborhood in the city of Salinas on the south coast, for example, were almost fully occupied before Maria. Eighteen months after the storm, almost none of the flood-damaged homes had yet been repaired, and three-fourths of all houses stood empty.[100] Left with only 25 percent of its members, a community such as Sierra Brava becomes even more vulnerable to the future economic shocks or climatic disasters that the island is likely to face.

Puerto Ricans condemned Trump's abuse, but they didn't stop there. Naomi Klein and others have documented the remarkable community initiatives that arose in Hurricane Maria's wake to build back sustainably and fend off the "disaster capitalists" and bitcoin billionaires who had swooped in after the storm like carrion crows.[101] And amazingly, despite unbearable economic stress, the territorial government jumped ahead of the U.S. mainland in climate action. In March 2018, the legislature passed the Puerto Rico Energy Public Policy Act, the island's own version of a Green New Deal. The Act requires the island to achieve a 40 percent renewable electricity supply by 2025 and 100 percent by 2050; ban coal-fired power plants by 2028; make it faster and easier for those with household solar arrays to connect to the grid and sell power into the system; and streamline the permitting of wind and solar installations. These are among a host of other provisions for climate mitigation and justice.[102]

Puerto Rico has drawn up an ambitious green blueprint. But how will its planned ten-year transformation of the energy infrastructure, including dramatic expansion of rooftop solar capacity, hold up if Maria-scale storms begin returning every five years, then every three? And even if Puerto Rico gets lucky, as it did in 2019 when Hurricane Dorian came close without making landfall, how can the territory build back better, while debt relief and federal disaster funding continue to be withheld?[103]

EMITTING THE LEAST, ENDURING THE WORST

Throughout 2017 and much of 2018, claims were flying that technological advances and market forces would make the elimination of fossil fuels inevitable. The Trump years, we were told, would not be as bleak as they seemed; it was only a matter of time before the private sector would completely eliminate its carbon emissions. During his last days in office, Barack Obama himself helped kick off this line of argument with an opinion piece published in *Science*, America's highest-profile research journal. In the article, daringly titled "The Irreversible Momentum of Clean Energy," Obama wrote, "Businesses are coming to the conclusion that reducing emissions is not just good for the environment—it can also boost bottom lines, cut costs for consumers, and deliver returns for shareholders." He argued that although strong public climate policy and leadership remained important, "technology advances and market forces will continue to drive renewable deployment" in the transformation to a climate-safe society.[104]

Six weeks into Trump's term, with federal environmental policy already going through the executive branch's paper shredders and wood chippers, a solar company executive told the tech news site *Engadget*, "Solar has the lowest cost of generation in many places, and when that statement can be made without the caveat of 'in many places,' then it'll be unstoppable." Confident in the face of a new administration that was in love with fossil fuels, he added, "There's no political or social force that can resist [lowering prices]. Not even the president of the United States can fight it."[105] Adnan Amin, the director general of the International Renewable Energy Agency, told *Forbes* in early 2018, "Turning to renewables for new power generation is not simply an environmentally conscious decision, it is now—overwhelmingly—a smart economic one. We expect the transition to gather further momentum around the world in 2018."[106]

Few at the time were questioning the spurious assumption that the very act of building new wind and solar energy capacity would drive fossil fuels out of the market and reduce emissions at the necessary pace. The evidence underlying that assumption was weak. Green energy investment was also doing nothing to right the environmental and economic wrongs that the fossil-fueled economy had inflicted on marginalized communities then living in shadows of power plants or recovering from wind, flood, or fire damage in Texas, Florida, Puerto Rico, or California. Clearly, the market for climate justice was nonexistent.

In his 2016 essay on climate action in the age of Trump, Arnold Shroder had urged activists who were focused primarily on climate and the fossil-fuel menace to join forces with people fighting back against racism, mass incarceration, and deportation; those resisting the growing impunity of police to harass and shoot at will; fighting for workers' rights; and carrying out many other struggles. Two years later, the Green New Deal's backers would attempt to do just that. And in between, there was the Poor People's Campaign.

In mid-December 2016, Reverend William J. Barber, who had come to national attention in 2013 leading Moral Monday rallies against the actions of North Carolina's right-wing state legislature, reminded a nation in the grip of a post-election hangover that we have a moral obligation to ensure racial, economic, social, and environmental justice in the United States. He wrote, "Without strong voices from the social gospel movement, there may have never been a New Deal. There would have been no Civil Rights Movement without the moral framework underneath the Civil Rights Movement. There would not have been a critique on poverty and unchecked capitalism, labor rights, health care, criminal justice reform, climate change, and raising the minimum wage, without a moral premise underneath it. Moral framing allows us to change the language."[107]

For forty days in May and June 2018, a Poor People's Campaign inspired by Reverend Barber revived the movement of that name led by Dr. Martin Luther King Jr. a half-century earlier. The new version was carried out not only in Washington, but also in thirty state capitals across the country. Local groups took to government offices and the streets to practice civil disobedience, and on each one of the six days of action, between 200 and 500 people were arrested around the nation.[108] As in King's campaign, these direct actions were aimed at ending systemic racism, poverty, and militarism. But in this new, perilous century, the movement had added a crucial new target: ecological devastation. Borrowing a term from Jaqui Patterson, the director of the

NAACP Environmental and Climate Justice Program, the Poor People's Campaign designated greenhouse warming in particular a "multiplier of injustice" that had to be handled as a crisis.

In a report titled *The Souls of Poor Folks* that reviewed the state of the nation fifty years after the original Poor People's Campaign, while foreshadowing the Green New Deal's vision, the campaign's organizers explained the link between the ecological crisis and the founding justice issues of 1968:

> Only a system rooted in inequality would allow a wealthy elite to profit from a business model that threatens the future of most of humanity, including marginalized populations in this country. In that sense, climate change is caused by systemic economic, social, and political inequality. Likewise, the effects of climate change, such as water scarcity in some regions and superstorms and floods in others, extreme heat, and sea level rise, have unequal impacts. The people who suffer the most from the effects of climate change contribute the least to its causes. . . . On average, low-income households in the U.S. consume much less energy per capita than high-income households, and are therefore responsible for less greenhouse gas pollution.[109]

From the Dakotas, Puerto Rico, and Washington, D.C., to state capitals coast to coast, something was brewing. The clamor was not just to stop ignoring the escalating climate crisis and fix it, but also to stop ignoring and fix the litany of chronic social problems connected to the same system at the root of the crisis.

IS IT TIME TO SAY SOMETHING SCARY?

As mentioned in the Introduction, in October 2018, the Intergovernmental Panel on Climate Change (IPCC) issued an eye-popping special report on the necessity of holding global greenhouse warming to 1.5°C or less. The IPCC had concluded that the emissions targets set in the

Paris Agreement were far too weak to keep the Earth below the 1.5° limit. Their bottom line: carbon emissions would have to be cut almost by half before 2030, and net-zero emissions would have to be achieved by 2050.[110]

According to Ezra Silk, the report sent a high-voltage pulse through the movement. "When the IPCC report came out," he said, "and we saw the reaction to it, it was clear to us that something had shifted within the collective consciousness. There seemed to be some kind of inflection point at which the professional climate communicators seemed to have abandoned this dogma around 'We're not going to say anything scary.' There seemed to be a dawning sense that climate change is here now. The social process seemed to be catching up to the ecological impact."[111] Very soon, all of this new energy converged through the idea of a Green New Deal.

But what kind of Green New Deal was it to be? *New York Times* columnist Thomas Friedman would claim credit for the original idea because he had used the now-famous three words in a 2007 column, but the Green New Deal he had described was nothing like what most climate activists were envisioning in 2018. Still characterizing his own proposal as "mean green" in 2019, Friedman wrote, "I believe there is only one thing as big as Mother Nature, and that is Father Greed—a.k.a., the market. I am a green capitalist."[112]

Clearly Friedman, with what we might call his "Greed New Deal," was not the muse that inspired the Green New Deal of 2018. But the term's lineage did go back at least a decade. In 2008, an assortment of environmental activists, economists, green-industry people, and academics had announced the formation of a Green New Deal Group in the United Kingdom that would respond to the meltdown of the world's economies then in progress. The group proposed financial reforms that included a green stimulus package aimed at a "massive" conversion to green energy.[113] In 2019, one of the group's founders, Colin Hines, looked back at the proliferation of Green New Deals that followed: "The idea had its year in the Keynesian sun when the world concentrated on massive public spending to prevent the collapse of the economic system and to fund job programs. [Then–U.K. prime minister] Gordon Brown, Barack Obama, and the United Nations Environment

Programme (UNEP) called for a Green New Deal, the Greens set up a European Green New Deal movement, and green NGOs supported the idea." But once it became clear that complete economic collapse had been averted, the fever broke, and enthusiasm for a Green New Deal tapered off.

The U.K.'s Green New Deal Group lived on nevertheless, and Hines gives it a good share of credit for the vision's recent revival in the country of the original New Deal. In February 2018, he recalled, "two U.S. researchers met the Green New Deal member and economist Ann Pettifor[114] and as a result decided to take the Green New Deal name and concept back to the U.S."[115] The researchers happened to be colleagues of Alexandria Ocasio-Cortez, who would make an upgraded Green New Deal armed with an agenda for economic, social, and racial justice the centerpiece of her successful 2018 run for the House of Representatives.

In September 2018, the polling and research group Data for Progress (which had been working on a project called "What the Hell Happened?," aimed at helping Democrats get over the trauma of 2016 by winning in 2018) published its own thirty-nine-page report on policy details for a Green New Deal.[116] Also during the fall campaign, a group called New Consensus formed for the purpose of creating the vision for such a plan. In 2019, this group would take the lead in developing the details of the Green New Deal.[117]

In January 2019, the group Extinction Rebellion mounted its first U.S. action.[118] XR, as members abbreviated it, had formed in the United Kingdom the previous year to demand, among other things, that the government "enact legally binding policy measures to reduce carbon emissions to net zero by 2025."[119] In that and other ways, their vision went beyond even that of the Green New Deal. For example, Extinction Rebellion would establish "legal rights for ecosystems to thrive and regenerate in perpetuity" and would repair "the effects of ongoing ecocide to prevent extinction of human and all species." Like The Climate Mobilization and the 2016 Democratic platform, members of Extinction Rebellion called for a wartime-like mobilization and a just transition. As with the Poor People's Campaign, their actions were centered on nonviolent direct action, including civil disobedience. Extinction Rebellion made headlines worldwide when, on November 17, 2018, a direct-action contingent of 6,000 people blocked London's five major bridges over the Thames River for several hours. More widespread disruption followed a few months later, in April 2019, during a worldwide "week of action." In a New York City "die-in" on April 17, 2019, members lay down in the street outside City Hall, shutting down traffic until the event was finally broken up by police, who arrested sixty-two people.[120] Although Extinction Rebellion didn't officially advocate for the Green New Deal at that time, they turned up the thermostat on the sense of emergency that was propelling it through U.S. politics.

Meanwhile, the Sunrise Movement was throwing its full weight into advocating for the plan. A political action group made up largely of young people, Sunrise was first formed to support climate-friendly Democratic candidates in 2018. After the election, its members turned to pressuring Congressional Democrats to support a Green New Deal. A week after the big victory in the House, they walked into the Capitol and occupied the office of Speaker-to-be Nancy Pelosi, delivering hand-written letters demanding serious climate action and protesting Pelosi's refusal to create a Select Committee for a Green New Deal. At one point, Ocasio-Cortez arrived and joined in. Fifty-one people ended up being arrested.[121] That same day, said Margaret Salamon, "I was in London at the headquarters of Extinction Rebellion, preparing with them to shut down the bridges in Central London. So there we were, watching the TV as Sunrise occupied Pelosi's office, and it was sort of surreal." This was before XR had started up in the United States, so, Salamon said, "People in the office were confused. Some were like, 'Did Extinction Rebellion go to Washington?'"[122] In the end, Pelosi did not permit the formation of a select committee.

Through 2019, support for the Green New Deal kept rolling in like Atlantic Coast breakers. On March 15, teenagers across the United States walked out of their classrooms, joining a worldwide throng of 1.4 million in a wave of "School Strikes for Climate Action."[123] The climate-strike tactic—inspired by the actions of the Swedish student Greta Thunberg, then 15 years old—had spread through European schools starting in the summer and autumn of 2018, and by the time of the March 15 rallies, it had reached North America. From coast to coast, school strikers joined in with the group Youth Climate Strikes, whose platform led off with its own thirteen-point version of the Green New Deal.[124] In preparing for March 15, the strikers drew support from the Sunrise Movement, Greenpeace, and prominent U.S. climate scientists.[125]

HOW THE GREEN NEW DEAL BLEW OPEN THE CLIMATE DEBATE

A joint Congressional resolution introduced on February 7, 2019, in the House as HR-109 by Alexandria Ocasio-Cortez and in the Senate as SR-59 by Ed Markey (D-Mass.), was titled "Recognizing the duty of the Federal Government to create a Green New Deal." (See Appendix 1.) The chief "Green" goal was to meet "100 percent of the power demand in the United States through clean, renewable, and zero-emission energy sources, including by dramatically expanding and upgrading renewable power sources and by deploying new capacity." To bring that goal within closer reach, the resolution aimed to reduce the amount of electricity the nation required. For example, it provided for "smart" power grids that could handle intermittent solar- and wind-generated electricity efficiently and called for high energy efficiency in all existing and new buildings.

The resolution required eliminating pollution and greenhouse gas emissions from manufacturing, agriculture, and transportation "as much as is technologically feasible." It also called for "biological carbon sequestration," that is, for expanding robust forests and grasslands that can draw carbon out of the atmosphere and store it in the soil, where it can't contribute to greenhouse warming.

The resolution's "New Deal"–like provisions were aimed at ensuring "prosperity and economic security for all people of the United States." They included the strengthening of organized labor, public investment in the economy, job creation, diversification and increased community ownership of local and regional industries, economic safety nets, and universal higher education. Perhaps most dramatically, the Green New Deal would guarantee "a job with a family-sustaining wage, adequate family and medical leave, paid vacations, and retirement security to all people of the United States."

In all of these initiatives, priority would go to vulnerable and deindustrialized communities "that may otherwise struggle with the transition away from greenhouse gas intensive industries." Crucially, all goals would be achieved through "democratic and participatory processes" that would "promote justice and equity by stopping current, preventing future, and repairing historic oppression of Indigenous communities, communities of color, migrant communities, deindustrialized communities, depopulated rural communities, the poor, low-income workers, women, the elderly, the unhoused, people with disabilities, and youth," who were referred to collectively as "frontline and vulnerable communities."

Aware that the New Deal of the 1930s had overlooked—and even furthered—some of America's more oppressive forces, including white supremacy, today's Green New Dealers propose to combat the sources of social injustice head-on. The 1930s Deal was aimed at rescuing an imploding economy. Today's Green New Deal is aimed at preventing ecological catastrophe while restructuring an economy that has increasingly benefited the few while exploiting the many.

Writing for *The Atlantic*, Robinson Meyer summed up the GND economic approach: "Above all, the Green New Deal is a leftist resurrection of federal industrial policy. It is not an attempt to control the private sector, according to its authors; it is a bid to collaborate with it. And it draws on a set of ideas with a rich American history, extending long before the great World War II mobilization to which the Green New Deal is regularly compared."[126]

POLITICO's Michael Grunwald examined the Green New Deal alongside the $90 billion green proto-plan contained in the stimulus package that President Barack Obama pushed through Congress in the depths of the Great Recession. Grunwald noted that while Obama used his response to the economic emergency to push green initiatives, GND activists were using their response to the environmental emergency to push progressive economic initiatives and social justice.[127]

Meanwhile, a group of *Jacobin* writers went all in, declaring, "Only a Green New Deal can save us from climate apocalypse. . . . The good news is that after decades of political marginalization, the socialist left is gaining momentum. The task is to link the upswell of political mobilization across the country, much of which is implicitly advancing GND principles, to the political savvy of the new wave of insurgent Democrats and an explicit, fleshed-out GND agenda."[128]

Adam Rogers wrote in a February 2019 article for *Wired*, "By pouring everything in [the climate, food, water, workplace, and other] silos into one bin, the Green New Deal attempts to build a new coalition. It seems crazy. But really, it's a last-chance amplification of smaller, incremental, hopeful changes already happening around the country—built into a broader vision for political change. Too wild? Maybe. As the dyed-in-the-wool hacks never say until after the balloons drop: Politics is the art of the impossible."[129]

The Green New Deal, with its more expansive social justice goals for society as a whole, not only was advanced by Alexandria Ocasio-Cortez and other progressive candidates but also drew support from throughout the climate movement and most of the left. For example, the organization 350.org, which had rallied for a Green New Deal as far back as 2008, backed the version proposed by Ocasio-Cortez. Founder Bill McKibben told Amy Goodman of *Democracy Now!*, "They've introduced this legislation [and for] the first time we've had an answer to climate change that's on the same scale as the problem itself. That's why it's important. It gets the scale right, and it understands that at this point we have to address [climate] alongside inequality, alongside the economic insecurity that people suffer from, that this is an enormous crisis, but also an opportunity to remake not just a broken planet, but a broken society."[130]

The idea of a Green New Deal was able to vault straight to the center of the climate discussion in 2018 because its proponents managed to steer it clear of approaches that are viewed by the corporate sector as threats to wealth accumulation and economic growth. It set aside regulation, carbon pricing, international obligations, punishment of polluters, or other policies that were anathema to corporate power and had always elicited that ubiquitous excuse for not taking action on climate: "It will hurt the economy." As a hybrid climate/economic plan that gave priority to fairness and inclusion, it was able to draw enthusiastic support from young people and many different social justice movements. But it also did not appear to pose an immediate threat to big business, aside from the coal and petroleum giants. To some, it appeared to resolve the quarter-century-old debate over "climate versus jobs"; restoring ecological stability, it was claimed, would create the jobs.

THERE'S A HOLE IN THE DEAL

Despite the fact that the proposed climate action poses no serious threat to business, corporations and the Right have attacked the Green New Deal from all the predictable angles—it's big government, it's socialism, it's a job killer. In seeking something specific to snipe at, Trump and his fans resorted to concocting a shadow Green New Deal that made for a scarier target. The president came up with some especially fanciful inventions. He charged that the legislation, if passed, would mean "no more airplanes, no more cows," would involve "trains to Europe, Hawaii and Australia," and would set a limit of one car per household.[131] But in his ignorance, Trump was unintentionally making some valid points. To achieve the deep, on-schedule emissions cuts called for by the plan would indeed require deep reductions in car and air travel, elimination of the feedlot-cattle industry, and many other profound changes in the consumer culture that has become synonymous with the American way of life. There were Green New Deal supporters who acknowledged that fact, but such deep changes did not make it into the joint Congressional resolution or the initial versions of the plan published by the think tanks.

Among many of those who saw some deficiencies in the Green New Deal vision, there emerged a general recognition that it should nevertheless be supported. After all, it was the only train that would be leaving the station for at least a couple of years. Because it was still a vision without many specifics, those who had reservations could still embrace it without seeming hypocritical. For example, the

Climate Mobilization threw its support behind the Green New Deal in February 2019 despite concerns that as then conceived, the plan did not address "the reality of humanity's overshoot of ecological limits in areas beyond greenhouse gases."[132] Giorgos Kallis, an environmental studies professor at Barcelona Autonomous University and an advocate for degrowth—restraining economies within ecological limits—wrote, "It is not as though the Green New Deal is an agenda designed to fight climate change alone—it is a green Left agenda that we should pursue even if there were no climate change. And we have to pursue it independently of whether or not it is 'good for the economy,' because we put people before the economy." But he added a note of caution. The Green New Deal vision, he wrote, "does not challenge head-on prevalent patterns of consumption."[133] And *Monthly Review* editor John Bellamy Foster, while supporting some of its key elements, said that "a radical Green New Deal is, at best, just the entry point to such wider, eco-revolutionary change."[134]

Kate Aronoff, who had co-authored *Jacobin*'s enthusiastic review of the Green New Deal, later pointed to a term that notably appeared nowhere in the Congressional resolution: "fossil fuel."[135] She wrote, "Fossil fuel usage and extraction have each continued to increase and show few signs of slowing down—particularly as the United States becomes a net exporter of fossil fuels. In other words, the good isn't out-competing the bad. In such a context, placing real constraints on coal, oil, and gas companies is the only way to ensure we can reach our climate goals." Greenpeace USA also noticed the omission. After expressing support for the jobs-and-justice portion of the resolution, the group's climate director said, "The fossil fuel industry will not transition willingly and on its own. . . . We must make every effort to phase out fossil fuels at the same time as we promote renewable energy if we're going to make it."[136]

The Indigenous Environmental Network, which works to protect the Earth from contamination and exploitation by applying Indigenous knowledge, has been among those to express the strongest concerns about the Green New Deal's shortcomings. In a statement published on its website, the organization declared:

From sea level rise to loss of land to food insecurities, Indigenous frontline communities and Tribal nations are already experiencing the direct impacts of climate change, and we are encouraged to see these congressional leaders take charge to help Indigenous communities and Tribal nations protect their homelands, rights, sacred sites, waters, air, and bodies from further destruction.

However, while we are grateful to see this support by the Representative and Senator, we remain concerned that unless some changes are made to the resolution, the Green New Deal will leave incentives by industries and governments to continue causing harm to Indigenous communities. Furthermore, as our communities who live on the frontline of the climate crisis have been saying for generations, the most impactful and direct way to address the problem is to keep fossil fuels in the ground. We can no longer leave any options for the fossil fuel industry to determine the economic and energy future of this country. And until the Green New Deal can be explicit in this demand as well as closing the loop on harmful incentives, we cannot fully endorse the resolution. We remain supportive of Representative Ocasio-Cortez and Senator Markey's aspirations and hope to be constructive partners in actualizing the goal of generating radical change in the fight to protect the sacredness of Mother Earth.[137]

Although the Green New Deal that was proposed in the 2019 resolution explicitly sets the goal of "meeting 100 percent of the power demand in the United States through clean, renewable and zero-emission energy sources," it does not include an effective strategy for directly and rapidly reducing greenhouse emissions through fossil-fuel restrictions. There was only the implicit assumption that public investment in technology and infrastructure would energize market forces to automatically drive down emissions.

Green New Deal policies were designed to enhance economic prosperity, but the joint resolution was silent on the subject of economic growth. It didn't list encouragement of growth among the Green New Deal's goals (although in its early statements New Consensus, the group that led the drafting of the full Green New Deal, did include economic growth among its goals). Green New Dealers also have not acknowledged that the growth imperative is the chief obstacle blocking the way to effective climate action now and over the past three decades.

Jason Hickel of the London School of Economics is a leading critic of the idea that economic growth can continue indefinitely without ecologically ruinous consumption of material resources. He points out that although there has been a rapid rise in annual world output of renewable energy since 2000, total energy demand has risen six times as fast. He writes, "We need to do everything we can to transition to clean energy, yes. But we'll only succeed if we reduce the amount of energy we consume in the first place, rather than continuing to grow it. The science is clear: scaling down material use must be at the core of the Green New Deal—and at the center of our climate policy."[138]

The need to eliminate fossil fuels and their emissions is paramount. But Hickel is going beyond that, urging that we must deeply reduce our use of energy and materials in order to succeed. Why is that? Aren't wind, solar, and other new energy sources coming along to satisfy future demand? Can't they maintain and increase our current energy consumption? The short answer is no. The full story is the subject of the next chapter.

3

⤜⟡⤛

THE ROAD TO CORNUCOPIA
ISN'T PAVED

"Why, then, have our political leaders failed for decades to act on climate change with the required urgency? Because our political system values the profits of the fossil fuel industry more than the livelihoods, homes, and the very lives of the poor."
—William Barber and Liz Theoharis, 2019[139]

In the hot, campaign-addled August of 2016, the prominent climate activist Bill McKibben published in *The New Republic* the most explicit appeal yet for a climate-saving effort modeled on the U.S. industrial achievements of 1940 to 1944. Declaring, "It's not that global warming is *like* a world war. It *is* a world war," McKibben called for immediate construction of 300 solar photovoltaic factories across America, and a similar number of wind-turbine factories.

Citing the example of a gigantic semiconductor plant that had recently been constructed in New Mexico, McKibben outlined some initial steps toward converting the nation to 100 percent renewable energy: "Pick a site with good roads and a good technical school nearby to supply the workforce; find trained local contractors who can deal with everything from rebar to HVAC; get the local permits; order long-lead-time items like I-beam steel; level the ground and excavate; lay foundations and floors; build walls, columns, and a roof; 'facilitate each of the stations for factory machine tooling with plumbing, piping, and electrical wiring'; and train a workforce of 1,500."[140] Build a factory. Manufacture equipment. Install. Repeat 600 times.

In recent years, blueprints for reducing greenhouse gas emissions have been focusing less on regulation and more on building solar and wind energy capacity. It goes without saying that if fossil fuels are to be flushed out of the national and world economies, alternative sources of energy will be required. But that logic doesn't work in reverse. Building new energy installations won't keep oil and gas in the ground or greenhouse gases out of the atmosphere. A Green New Deal–style new-energy buildup is essential, but it has to be complemented by direct mechanisms to phase out fossil fuels and drive emissions down to zero.

In the next chapter, I'll discuss such mechanisms, how they can help bring about the fair and just transition called for by the Green New Deal, and how we all can play important roles in achieving the transition. I'll be arguing that doing so will require our society to undergo sweeping systemic change. That's a lot to ask, so I begin by presenting the growing body of evidence that demonstrates why more cautious approaches, ones that would employ technical fixes, market competition, carbon pricing, and other seemingly simple solutions, aren't enough to prevent ecological catastrophe and the social destabilization being forecast by scientists. We need to stop using fossil fuels, and do so by a clear date.

100 PERCENT WISHFUL THINKING

McKibben based his climate-war proposal on a paper published the previous year by Mark Jacobson of Stanford University and his colleagues. The article purported to show, state by state, how the United States could replace fossil fuels and meet all future energy demand using only solar, wind, and hydroelectric generation.[141] It was one of a stream of articles by several groups outlining scenarios in which various combinations of wind, solar, geothermal, hydroelectric, and bioenergy capacity could supply 100 percent of our energy needs. A climate movement weary of a steady diet of bad news was invigorated by the reassuring picture painted in the scenarios. But nipping at those reports' heels came study after study pointing out the serious flaws in all the 100 percent renewable plans.[142]

A 2017 paper by a group of Australian researchers rated the feasibility of twenty-four published research papers describing 100 percent renewable scenarios at regional, national, and global scales. They concluded that among those studies (several of them with Jacobson as lead author), none "provides convincing evidence that . . . basic feasibility criteria can be met." They found a wide range of technical flaws in the proposed systems: deeply unrealistic assumptions about future improvements in energy efficiency; failure to compensate fully for the fact that a wind farm or solar park can't pour energy into the grid around the clock or on demand, as coal- and gas-fired power plants can; and lack of a means for preventing the kinds of voltage and frequency fluctuations that can wreak havoc throughout the electric grid. This and more added up, they wrote, to a "fragile" system that fails to deliver the promised output of electricity when it is needed.[143]

A few weeks later, the journal *Proceedings of the National Academy of Sciences* (*PNAS*) published an analysis by Christopher Clack and twenty co-authors critiquing a 2015 Jacobson paper setting out a plan for an all-renewable U.S. energy supply (a companion paper to the one that had inspired McKibben.) The Clack team took aim at the paper's proposals for sweeping deployment of technologies that either don't yet exist or have been only lightly tested and are highly unlikely to be feasible at the massive scales required. For example, they concluded that the Jacobson group's scenario "makes unsupported assumptions about widespread adoption of hydrogen as an energy carrier, including the conversion of the aviation and steel industries to hydrogen and the ability to store in hydrogen an amount of energy equivalent to more than 1 month of current US electricity consumption . . ." and also assumes that every building in America will be fitted with a technology called underground thermal energy storage, which has never been shown to work on a large scale.[144] A couple of years earlier, another U.S. group of analysts had examined seventeen published papers (again including some of Jacobson's) that outlined strategies for fully replacing fossil fuels with renewable energy and found that they all lacked the scientific rigor to be reliable guides for policymaking in the real world.[145]

Shaky as it was, the 100 percent renewable vision gave mainstream activists what they needed to cut through the gloom emanating from melting glaciers and deliver the energizing message that we can do something about the climate emergency. In that, it has been useful, giving efforts to secure Green New Deal–style public investment for the buildout of non-fossil energy capacity a much-needed shot in the arm. But the 100 percent narrative has hurt the broader climate effort by creating unrealistic expectations that could backfire down the road, while drawing attention and energy away from the need for direct, rapid reductions in fossil fuel use, starting immediately.

ABUNDANT GREEN ENERGY
(FOR SOME OF US)

The Green New Deal focuses on the U.S. economy, and rightly so: Congress can legislate domestically, but its only effective way to lead on climate stabilization globally is by example. Still, if it were possible to achieve the goal of providing 100 percent renewable energy for 100 percent of current and growing U.S. demand, what might happen in the rest of the world? The Jacobson team was ready with an answer. Having declared victory in the domestic climate war, they published a 2017 paper claiming to show that 139 countries encompassing the bulk of Earth's human population also would be able to satisfy all future energy demand with only wind, solar, and hydroelectric energy.[146] There was just one hitch. Billions of people around the world need more energy than they can afford, billions of others can buy far more energy than is required to meet their needs, and the paper's 100 percent renewable scenario implicitly accepted that those deep social inequalities will persist long into the future.

It is estimated that for societies to achieve minimum satisfactory levels of human development, they need a combination of energy sources that can deliver a flux of about 1,300 watts per person.[147] Some estimates go higher; in Switzerland, a two-decade-old project aims toward a modest "2,000-watt society."[148] But for a large share of humanity, Jacobson and co-authors set their sights lower than 2,000 W or even 1,300 W. Here are the targets for per-capita consumption that their global roadmap would try to meet with renewable energy in a few of the continents, regions, and countries they examined (compare these with a whopping 9,500 W currently available per person in the United States and approximately 5,000 W in Europe):[149]

South America	1,413 W
Southeast Asia	1,007 W
Africa	625 W
India	755 W
Haiti	760 W
Cuba	705 W

Jacobson and colleagues tried to justify these skimpy energy allotments by assuming that all nations will not only convert to renewable energy, but also become super-efficient in their energy consumption. That way, they just won't need much. But such expectations are unrealistic even for rich countries, let alone those that are struggling to pull themselves out of poverty. Researchers at Germany's Potsdam Institute for Climate Impact Research have concluded that impoverished nations striving to achieve higher levels of human development will not be able to achieve rapid improvements in energy efficiency at the same time. Whether or not stoves and refrigerators can be made to run on less energy, they argue, the society-wide infrastructure improvements necessary for development—involving as they do a lot of inputs like cement and steel—will continue to require massive inputs of energy.[150] And most countries don't have the money to do that and at the same time replace fossil fuels with new energy sources.

A nation currently operating at only half of the aforementioned 1,300 W threshold for satisfactory human development, as Jacobson and colleagues are asking India, Haiti, Cuba, and the whole continent of Africa to continue to do, will need a big inflow of resources if it is to achieve sufficiency for all and at the same time reduce greenhouse emissions. And while developing new capacity for energy and general development, they will need to *increase* their fossil-fuel consumption for a while. To compensate, wealthy countries will have to reduce their own fossil fuel use even more steeply.[151]

Here in the United States, accepting either the IPCC deadlines for driving down greenhouse emissions, the Green New Deal's goals, or any other ambitious emissions targets would effectively fix the rate at which fossil-fuel consumption will have to be reduced year by year. Then the question will be whether new energy sources can be brought on line fast enough to substitute for the fossil energy that's being eliminated from the economy. The prospects are not good. For example, Jacobson's U.S. plan would require installation of wind and solar electric capacity at fifteen times the annual rate at which new electric capacity from all sources was installed over the past half-century.[152] Substituting energy from wind, solar, and hydroelectric for all energy derived from liquid fossil fuels and gas- and coal-fired power plants by 2030, as espoused by some Green New Deal advocates, would mean building solar and wind infrastructure at thirty-three times the highest rate of buildup ever achieved to date.[153] No such growth rates are reachable. If consumption of fossil fuel declines at the necessary rate over the next one to three decades, the total U.S. energy supply is going to shrink for a while.

Maybe America should regard the contraction of our total energy supply as an opportunity, accept the idea that we don't need an input of almost 10,000 W per capita, and decide that we could have a better quality of life if we were consuming far less energy. Then we could aim to diminish fossil-fuel use even faster, since we would need to fill only a portion of the resulting energy gap with renewable sources. It would also mean that a lot less of the nation's energy and resources would be poured into constructing and operating a whole new power grid. And billions that would not be spent on maintaining an excessive energy supply could be used to support the efforts of resource-poor regions of the world to meet human needs while replacing fossil fuels with renewable sources. Doing all of that would not only achieve steeper emissions reductions but also be a start toward greater justice in the world's energy and economic systems.

ELECTRIC SPRAWL

Getting fossil fuels out of our lives will not only be climate-friendly, but will also end the environmental damage that comes with extracting and burning coal, crude, and gas. We can say goodbye to underwater drilling, "fracking" (hydraulic fracturing), strip mining of coal and tar sands, refining, and methane leakage. But it's impossible to acquire industrially produced energy of any kind without doing ecological damage. The impacts of wind and solar generation on local ecosystems are less intensive than those of fossil fuel extraction, but wind farms and solar parks will need to occupy far more acreage than oil or gas wells in order to supply the same total quantity of energy. Any industrial installation has a disruptive effect on the landscape where it sits; inevitably, a high-energy global economy powered by 100 percent renewable sources covering hundreds of millions of acres would have far-reaching ecological impacts.

Consider solar energy. Given the unfathomably large quantity of sunlight striking the Earth's surface, expectations for almost unlimited energy production would seem at first glance to be justified. But the incoming solar irradiation is very diffuse. To collect a quantity of such energy sufficient to run an entire economy will require efforts far more extensive, difficult, and complicated than civilization became accustomed to during the fossil-fuel era.[154]

Taking all physical and practical limitations into account, the applied physicist Carlos de Castro and his colleagues at the University of Valladolid in Spain calculate that even if the future brings unexpectedly rapid technological advances, most of the 100 percent renewable scenarios would require solar installation on at least as many square miles of the Earth's surface as are now occupied by all food production and human settlement combined. One of Jacobson's scenarios would use more than three times as much land as is now used for agriculture.[155] The amount of energy in the Earth's winds is also enormous, but about 80 percent of them blow across landscapes that are inaccessible or places where it's not possible or advisable to construct a wind farm. And only half of the remaining area is sufficiently windy to justify the energy and effort that would go into installing and operating the farm. Generating a significant portion of the energy supply with wind would occupy immense acreages.[156] It plays a major role in Jacobson's U.S. plan for 100 percent renewable energy, to the extent that wind farms would need to cover 6 percent of the entire land surface of the forty-eight contiguous states.[157]

Covering vast tracts of the Earth's surface with energy-harvesting equipment could not be done without inflicting environmental harm. Patrick Moriarty and Damon Honnery of Monash University in Australia argue that all energy generation has ecological side effects that, if left unaddressed, will undermine efforts to generate and use the energy needed to build and maintain a green society.[158] Some large portions of the Earth's surface should be ruled out for energy production altogether, because the ecological damage done by encroaching on those landscapes would cancel out the environmental benefits of producing nominally carbon-free energy. In other areas, a smaller degree of environmental damage may be judged an acceptable and necessary price to pay, but it still must be acknowledged and accounted for.

The energy and money required to build wind and solar facilities is spent almost entirely up front. But the environmental impacts of a solar park or wind farm unfold throughout and beyond its functional lifetime. Our future depends on protecting the land areas of the Earth that have not yet been built upon or plowed, and restoring the lands and waters we have already degraded.[159] There is no way to cover more land with solar parks than we cover with crops, or to place wind farms on one square mile out of every sixteen in the United States, without causing serious ecological disruption.

Other environmental side effects of solar generation include pollution from solar photovoltaic (PV) factories, water consumption for washing dust from PV panels in places where fresh water is already scarce, and reducing the albedo (reflectivity) of the Earth's surface, which will compound the greenhouse effect and accelerate warming. Expansion of wind capacity will mean an escalating death toll among birds and bats, while offshore wind farms would also threaten marine mammals and coastal ecosystems in general.[160] This isn't to say that we should not build solar and wind capacity; rather, we should build as much as is needed to run an energy-frugal society, not an energy-gluttonous one, and do it in places where ecological damage can be minimized.

GREEN REVERIES

Could we shrink the human footprint on much of the Earth by retreating into cities? The folks at the Oakland, California–based Breakthrough

Institute think so. In their 2015 "Ecomodernist Manifesto,"[161] they argued that if we pursue unrestrained economic and technological growth, implausibly big gains in food productivity, and extreme urbanization, humanity could leave much of the natural world free to flourish and make "more room for non-human species." Energy for pulling off this grand experiment would be provided largely by nuclear fission and, if it becomes feasible, hydrogen fusion.

While disparaging (on no specific grounds) the Club of Rome's concept of limits to growth (see Chapter One), the manifesto was littered with extraordinary claims such as these, none of them supported by empirical evidence:

To the degree to which there are fixed physical boundaries to human consumption, they are so theoretical as to be functionally irrelevant.

There is still remarkably little evidence that human population and economic expansion will outstrip the capacity to grow food or procure critical material resources in the foreseeable future.

Humans are as likely to spare nature because it is not needed to meet their needs as they are to spare it for explicit aesthetic and spiritual reasons.

Cities both drive and symbolize the decoupling of humanity from nature, performing far better than rural economies in providing efficiently for material needs while reducing environmental impacts.

At its most fanciful, ecomodernism takes the form of "Fully Automated Luxury Communism," a future in which all work is performed by robots, so that human labor is no longer exploited, and everyone receives a good income. Its leading proponent, Aaron Bastani, sums it up as "the full automation of everything and common ownership of that which is automated." Gene editing, lab-cultured meat, artificial intelligence, asteroid mining, and 3-D printing all will play roles in this "post-scarcity society." And yes, it has its own manifesto, a book-length one by Bastani.[162]

In a rebuttal of the original Ecomodernist Manifesto, a group of eighteen authors, including well-known ecologists and ecological economists, argued that all available evidence goes against the eco-modernists' claim that production, consumption, and wealth can increase without limit and with no negative environmental consequences. Their argument criticizes the manifesto for engaging in a romanticized, nineteenth-century-style worship of industrial progress, exaggerating the benefits and ignoring its harsh impacts on people and the Earth; that ecomodernism would mean "leaving the developing world to play an impossible game of catch-up with levels of energy and material consumption in the developed world"; that the ecomodernists treat rural and Indigenous cultures with condescension and disdain; and that the manifesto made naïve claims that larger, denser cities can somehow supply themselves with food and consume vast quantities of resources with no ecological impact while providing superior quality of life to the people crowding into them.[163]

The rebuttal noted that even if we could disregard all of the above, the whole ecomodernist enterprise is undermined by its all-out embrace of nuclear power and listed eight of the well-known environmental and geopolitical reasons why nuclear is so dirty and dangerous that it must be ruled out.[164] In a 2018 piece titled "Where's the 'Eco' in Ecomodernism?" for the site *Red Pepper*, Aaron Vansintjan piled on with other crucial considerations that seal the case against nuclear: "The problem with nuclear clearly isn't technical, it's political. The prospect of scaling up nuclear to the level needed to replace fossil fuels begs two questions. First, are our political institutions robust enough? Second, do we want the world that nuclear creates? A world full of nuclear power plants is a world of highly centralized power, an energy system removed from people by an army of specialized engineers and, to protect it, a maximum-security state. To think that any technology can be grabbed out of the current system and scaled up without consequences is a profoundly un-ecological idea."[165]

In 2018, *Vox*'s David Roberts discussed a new *PNAS* report in which four scientists concluded that, like it or not, the nuclear power industry will be "vanishing" in coming decades. Roberts deemed the paper "remarkable because it is *not* written by opponents of nuclear power, as one might expect given the conclusion. The authors are in fact extremely supportive of nuclear and view its loss as a matter of 'profound concern.'"[166] These experts foresaw grim prospects for the industry, writing that "because of their great cost and complexity, it appears most unlikely that any new large [conventional nuclear] plants will be built over the next several decades. While advanced reactor designs are sometimes held up as a potential solution to nuclear power's challenges, our assessment of the advanced fission enterprise suggests that no US design will be commercialized before midcentury."[167] Of course, by midcentury, it will be too late; the question of whether or not intensification of global warming can be stopped will already have been answered. The scientists concluded that the only nearer-term possibility could be so-called small modular reactors (SMRs); however, they wrote, "We have systematically investigated how a domestic market could develop to support that industry over the next several decades and, in the absence of a dramatic change in the policy environment, have been unable to make a convincing case."

For all their dreams of wholly reconfiguring a society's geographical layout and its means of provisioning itself, ecomodernists have had nothing to say about system change, and they mount no challenge to the status quo. The ecological economists' response to the manifesto concluded that "ecomodernism offers a peculiarly whitewashed and sugary interpretation of industrial modernism, and fails to acknowledge that the interrelated problems of overconsumption and environmental decline were *not* coincidental by-products of those modern industrial processes. Industrial modernity has certainly brought numerous benefits to humankind, but it has come at a heavy toll, and one that jeopardizes the possibility of creating a sustainable society."

The ecomodernists claim that breakneck growth is necessary if we are to develop the means to prevent climatic ruin. But the real arrow of intent points the other way. Their proposed policies are meant to maintain growth at all costs, while environmental benefits are simply assumed into existence. And the fantasy that economic growth will turn not only San Francisco and Dallas but also Karachi, Kampala,

Tegucigalpa, and hundreds of other big, economically stressed cities of the global South into ecomodern powerhouses ignores the fact that growth here in the North has always depended upon exploitation of the South. The already struggling nations of the South don't have that option; they aren't going to achieve limitless growth by exploiting themselves. No city, rich or poor, can accumulate wealth without limit.[168]

WHEN NIGHT DESCENDS
AND BREEZES CALM

As futurists carry on with their daydreams of mining ores out of asteroids, scientists and engineers here on Earth continue their dogged search for a way to supply humanity's energy needs from wind and solar sources. The most vexing problem is that nowhere does the wind blow or the sun shine brightly around the clock, every day of the year. Coal- and gas-fired plants can send out a continuous flow of power day and night, and gas can be dialed up or down quickly at any time in response to changing demand. On the other hand, a wind farm's output at any given moment is determined not by demand but by how hard the wind is blowing at that instant.

The intermittency of sunlight and wind energy is not a problem when wind farms and solar parks are contributing a small share of the electricity supply and feed into the same power grid as coal and gas plants. But if the share of electricity supplied by wind and solar rises beyond 25 and 50 percent toward 100 percent, as is envisioned by the Green New Deal and other ambitious green-energy scenarios, the grid will have to deal with more and bigger supply gaps than can be filled by the dwindling numbers of gas-fired plants. Therefore, most plans envision storing large amounts of wind and solar energy when it's not needed and using it later. Then, for example, excess electricity generated on a sunny, windy December day in Kansas could be accumulated and dispatched later that night to heat homes in a frigid Chicago. Storage is needed not only to match up local supply and demand throughout the system but also to cover for large-scale power outages caused by severe weather or other factors.[169]

William Pickard, a professor of electrical engineering at Washington University in St. Louis, asks us to imagine an "affluent but frugal society" living on 5,000 W per capita, equitably distributed. For this illustration, let's say that society is a future, more egalitarian United States consuming half as much energy per person as today's does. To protect every part of that nation against a two-day outage would mean building and hooking up to the grid 240 kilowatt-hours per capita of storage capacity. Is that a lot? What would it look like? To visualize that amount of storage, Pickard did some rough calculations and translated them into vivid, pre-industrial images. It could be done, he says, by manufacturing and installing twenty thousand pounds of lithium-ion batteries per person in the United States. If gathered in one place (which in practice they wouldn't be), the batteries would occupy the volume of five hundred Great Pyramids of Giza and weigh more than 6 trillion pounds. In what promise to be disaster-filled decades ahead, Pickard deems it preferable to have not two days' but rather two weeks' storage capacity in place to deal with widespread, prolonged outages, but that wouldn't be possible. The batteries required for two weeks' storage would weigh 42 trillion pounds and match the volume of 3,500 Giza pyramids.[170]

Trillions of pounds of batteries would have an unbearably heavy environmental impact, and, Pickard advises, no current battery technology can be counted upon to perform optimally at such an ambitious scale. Alternative storage ideas include using excess wind and solar energy to compress air into underground chambers or pump water uphill into reservoirs and let it rush down through hydroelectric turbines later when power is needed. Of these and other proposed storage systems, Pickard writes, "They should work, but the history of technology is littered with the ruins of major projects that failed because of unanticipated consequences."

The problem of intermittent wind and sunlight could be largely resolved and the need for batteries reduced if gaps in energy supply were filled by non-fossil-fuel power plants that could be turned up or down as needed. Therefore, Jacobson and colleagues relied on extraordinary quantities of hydroelectric power in their scenarios, despite the well-known damage that dams and reservoirs can do to rivers and ecosystems and the displacement of human communities and livelihoods they can cause. Even if we were to accept such damage, there are only so many locations suitable for hydropower, so there's a relatively low ceiling on the amount of energy that can be obtained by that route. Therefore, most plans put forward by IPCC reports and many academic papers have looked to biomass—stems and leaves of grasses, wood from forests, or general cellulosic waste materials—as a flexible source of carbon-based energy that, like coal, can be stockpiled and then burned whenever it's needed.

Here's the plan. Green plants pull global-warming CO_2 out of the atmosphere. The plants are harvested, dried and pelletized. Electric utilities burn the pellets, adding to the national energy supply. That releases the CO_2 that the plants originally pulled out of the air, but the CO_2 is not allowed back into the air; the utilities will capture and bury it before it leaves the chimney.

This process, called bioenergy with carbon capture and storage (BECCS), looks at first glance like a win-win solution. We get electricity when and where it's needed, day or night, and the atmosphere gets less CO_2. But BECCS stumbles on both counts, delivering less electricity and burying less carbon than promised. Before the energy generated by the biomass-fueled plant goes into the grid, large quantities of other energy will already have been consumed to grow and harvest the crop, haul the biomass to a processing plant, transform it into pellets, haul the pellets to the power plant, capture the CO_2 emitted when the pellets are burned, convert the CO_2 into a liquid or other portable form, haul it to an abandoned oil or gas well, and inject it under high pressure. Those energy expenditures together will cancel out 25 to 100 percent of the energy produced by the BECCS plant. If the energy for growing and hauling the crops is provided by fossil fuels (as would be the case well into the future) part of the carbon-capture benefits also will be canceled out.[171]

(What if instead of pulling CO_2 out of a coal- or biomass-fueled power plant, we were to take it directly out of the atmosphere, thereby reducing the pace of global warming? This process, known as direct-air capture, may be of interest in the future if we find, after accomplishing a full conversion to non-fossil energy, that we have failed to meet emission-control targets and need to reduce the atmospheric CO_2 concentration. However, it is not a substitute for emissions reduction and should not be attempted before all greenhouse-gas sources have been eliminated. The technology is not safely applicable at large scale[172], and even if it were, the ability to pull lots of CO_2 out of the air would create an irresistible temptation to extend the use of fossil fuels, putting the world on a dead-end treadmill. Direct-air capture also has huge energy requirements, which, if met with fossil fuels, could fully cancel out its climate benefits.[173])

Production of the crops to be fed into BECCS not only would require a lot of energy but would also do far-reaching social and ecological damage. To pull less than 10 percent of humanity's annual CO_2 emissions out of the atmosphere would require bioenergy plantations covering one-third as much land as is already used to grow food, feed, and fiber crops. That pressure on a fixed land supply would drive up the costs of basic foodstuffs, imperiling the food security of billions of people. Growing that much fuel biomass would consume water in huge quantities similar to those used to irrigate food crops today, deepening the water crisis for billions around the globe. One-fifth or more of natural forests, grasslands, and savannahs could be lost, wiping out more biodiversity than would a global temperature rise of 2.8°C (5°F) above pre-industrial levels—the very scale of disaster that the bioenergy push is aimed at preventing. Bringing vast new acreages of land under cultivation will break down organic matter in soils, releasing CO_2 into the atmosphere and canceling out a big portion of what's being captured. In fact, if very large natural landscapes are brought into bioenergy production, all of its carbon-capture benefits could be wiped out; the whole project could become a net carbon emitter.[174] For these and other reasons, Jacobson and colleagues wisely left BECCS out of their 100 percent renewable scenarios, and it did not appear in the Green New Deal resolution.

Neither batteries nor biomass can bring back the days of easy energy. It is eminently feasible for a U.S. economy to operate without fossil fuels, but it will have to run on much less total energy—and it will have to be a very different kind of economy.

WHO HYPED THE ELECTRIC CAR?

The 100 percent renewable scenarios can be made to work out on paper only by assuming historically unprecedented, technically unrealistic increases in energy efficiency. Some call for efficiency improvements in the coming decades that would be faster than, and sometimes twice as fast as, any achieved so far.[175] The optimists call for these brisk rates to be sustained over several decades through the all-out pursuit of new technologies. At the top of most optimists' lists of exciting new products is the electric car.[176]

The electric vehicle has captured the imagination of renewable-energy planners because on average it consumes less energy per mile than a car with a gas or diesel engine. An all-electric car and truck fleet the same size as the current fleet theoretically running on less energy would lighten the demand on tomorrow's renewable-energy industry. Electric vehicles, the thinking goes, will hold down the number of wind farms and solar parks that will have to be built, the miles of transmission lines that will have to be strung, and the tonnage of storage batteries that will be needed to electrify and "de-carbonize" personal transportation.

The situation is much more complicated than the optimists acknowledge. If we're talking about the energy savings from driving an electric car in the 100 percent renewable world of the future, we need to account not just for the energy required to move a car or truck down the road but also the energy that's burned in the extraction of minerals and production of materials that go into it, and in its manufacture and eventual disposal. Largely because of its big battery, an electric car requires more than twice as much energy in its production than an internal-combustion car.[177] Full-electrification scenarios would send America's 250 million gas- and diesel-fueled cars and trucks to the junkyard and replace all of them with electric vehicles within a decade or two. Doing so would require that a huge quantity of energy be expended in mines, smelters, and factories long before the energy savings advertised for electric vehicles could be realized. And during the first ten or twenty years at least (the same climate-emergency decades in which we need to dramatically reduce greenhouse emissions), much of the electricity used to make and drive electric cars will continue to be provided by fossil fuels.

The ecological consequences of manufacturing electric vehicles extend well beyond greenhouse warming. Industrial ecologists have identified many production impacts that are as bad as or much worse than the impacts of gas and diesel cars, including acidification of terrestrial and marine ecosystems; emissions of air pollutants in addition to CO_2; water pollution; and toxicity to humans and other species. The potential for human toxicity in particular is off the charts. Most of the electric vehicles' ecological damage would result from increased mining and processing of nickel, copper, aluminum, and other metals required for electric vehicles' big batteries and other parts.[178] Those impacts have not yet been widely noticed, because so few electric vehicles have so far been manufactured and sold. Pointing out the tiny numbers of electric cars purchased in recent years relative to internal-combustion vehicles, *Washington Post* columnist Charles Lane argues that as long as electrics require frequent, time-consuming recharge and carry a high price tag, they will remain "a niche product for upper-income folks."[179]

The replacement of current coal- and gas-fired electric generation with non-fossil energy sources is going to be a very steep hill to climb. If sales of electric vehicle do eventually surge, they, along with other power-hungry additions such as electric space heating (required to replace gas heating) and rapidly expanding digital communications, will dramatically increase the demand that the power grid will be expected to satisfy, putting more and more obstacles in the road to 100 percent renewable electricity. We have no choice but to make hard decisions about what we will and won't try to do. For example, replacing gas- and oil-fired furnaces with electric heat pumps will be necessary, but we can no longer support a car and a pickup in every driveway, however they are powered.[180]

METAL MADNESS

There are twenty-three minerals critical to the coming manufacturing boom that would supply the electric grid and electric vehicle fleet as well as components for wind turbines, solar arrays, high-speed rail, and other features of the new infrastructure. The boom's requirements will intensify the current global rush for a broad range of metals, including lithium, cobalt, silver, copper, aluminum, nickel, iron, and the exotic rare earth elements cerium, lanthanum, dysprosium, neodymium, and praseodynum.[181]

A group of analysts in Australia and Japan estimated the total quantities of various metals that would be required between now and 2050 in order to create a world mostly powered by renewable electricity. They concluded that such a world would probably run out of cobalt and lithium well before 2050. Even with recycling of metals, the quantity of cobalt required for battery manufacture would equal 120 to 210 percent of all known reserves on Earth, while 90 to 160 percent of all lithium reserves would be required.[182]

Mining is always a nasty business. The world's cobalt deposits are concentrated in central Africa, largely in the Democratic Republic of the Congo (DRC), and its extraction is taking a terrible human toll, whether in big corporate operations or individual wildcat mines. Cobalt is highly toxic, and miners, often children, wear little or no protective gear. Extracting lithium carbonate from salt flats at the intersection of Argentina, Chile, and Bolivia—one of the driest regions on Earth—requires a half-million gallons of water per metric ton of lithium, as well as hydrochloric acid and various toxic chemicals that have leaked into the area's scant water supplies. Amit Katwala reported for *Wired*, "In Chile, there have been clashes between mining companies and local communities, who say that lithium mining is leaving the landscape marred by mountains of discarded salt and canals filled with contaminated water with an unnatural blue hue."[183]

Since 2015, when the Chinese government called for a rapid buildup of the country's fleet of electric cars, hundreds of lithium-mining projects have been launched. One such operation has caused repeated fish kills in the Liqi River in Sichuan Province, and cattle and yaks that drank from the river also have died.[184] The majority of the world's rare-earth mining currently occurs in China, with devastating environmental impacts across the country. Soil and water pollution resulting from rare-earth mining and processing was killing crops in Inner Mongolia as early as 1980. Today in Mongolia, a hamlet located near a rare-earth mine and tailing pond is known as a "death village." Its high rates of cancer and other diseases may be related to radioactive elements present in the ore.[185]

The ecological damage humanity has done over the past two centuries in the quest for fossil fuels could easily be reprised in the damage caused by the stampede to accumulate raw materials for the new energy and transportation economy. The bulk of the world's reserves of critical metals lies outside U.S. borders, so the mining impacts of fully electrifying our economy will be felt largely in other countries. And, just as America's past desperation to satisfy its outsize energy appetite with fossil fuels has led to economic oppression and military conflict around the globe, a future desperation to keep wind, solar, and battery factories supplied with resources being dug up on other continents could bring oppression and conflict. As *Green Social Thought* editor Don Fitz asked in 2014,

> Would the Green World Order mean that Venezuela might have less reason to fear an invasion aimed at gaining access to its heavy oils? Or, would it mean an additional invasion of Bolivia to grab its lithium for green batteries? Would northern Africa no longer need to fear attacks to secure Libyan oil? Or, would new green armies to secure solar collectors for European energy be added to existing armies? Across the globe, those marching with the red, white and blue banner of the War for Oil would continue to invade. But they could be joined by those marching with a green banner.[186]

Even if they refrain from intervening militarily, will the governments of affluent countries, eager for abundant green energy, become even more tolerant of abuses committed by corporations and governments in poverty-stricken but resource-rich regions? Recent history says yes. Of all internal conflicts suffered by the world's nations between 1950 and 2009, 40 percent were connected to natural-resource extraction.[187] Mining industries are notorious for endangering workers and ruining local environments, as well as engaging in land theft, conflict over access to deposits, and undermining of local economies.[188] In its 2018 report *Green Conflict Minerals*, the Winnipeg-based International Institute for Sustainable Development found that "the extraction and trade of mineral resources can fuel grievances, tensions and conflict, particularly when they happen in a context defined by weak governance, multidimensional poverty, human rights violations and youth unemployment."[189]

The report notes that the notorious cobalt-mining industry in the Democratic Republic of Congo has been "connected to child labor, dangerous working conditions, extortion, and human rights abuses." Of twenty-six manufacturers of electronic devices and electric cars surveyed by Amnesty International in 2017, none had sought to find out if human rights abuses were occurring during the mining or processing of the cobalt they were obtaining from the Republic. Meanwhile, forced displacement, murder, and sexual violence have been alleged to occur around the largest nickel mine in Central America, which is located near a Lote Ocho Indigenous community in Guatemala. Elsewhere in the country, says the report, members of the Maya Q'eqchi' community sued the mining company HudBay, alleging that private security personnel forced them to move off of ancestral lands, burned homes, and sexually assaulted women.

MONEY FOR NOTHING?

The past two centuries have proven, says the Land Institute's founder Wes Jackson, that "highly dense energy destroys information, both cultural and biological."[190] (As an example, Jackson points to the way in which agricultural mechanization, fertilizers, and other chemicals, all made possible by the energy concentrated in fossil fuels, have enabled the widespread cultivation of industrial crop monocultures, which harbor only a tiny fraction of biological information in the form of species richness and genetic diversity that would be found in either natural ecosystems or pre-industrial farms. Likewise lost, he notes, is the vast, complex cultural information that enabled communities to function and produce food before fossil fuels.) Large available reserves of mineral energy have been essential factors in the planetary-scale ecological degradation that is still in progress. Instead of liberating people from work, dense energy has helped intensify the exploitation of labor and accelerate the disruption of human relationships. If the world did somehow succeed in building enough nominally green energy capacity to fully replace the energy available today, and then kept building more, the new forms of energy would likely continue to perpetuate forms of cultural and biological deterioration.

Richard York of the University of Oregon has long wrestled in his research with the political economy of energy and ecology. "It's amazing," he told me. "Twenty years ago, I could never have imagined that a Green New Deal would come along and expand the domain of U.S. politics as it has. I was pleased to see its recognition that dealing with the climate crisis requires strong, concerted government effort. That's the plus part. But while it's much more radical than the mainstream climate movement, it's not radical enough. People don't want to think or talk about having less energy. And that's what we need."[191]

In climate plans that focus on a buildup of renewable energy, there is typically an implicit assumption (at times openly expressed) that the renewable energy capacity coming on line each year will be matched by an equivalent amount of coal-, oil-, or gas-fired capacity going off line. It would happen naturally, the reasoning goes, because renewable energy would be cheaper and more desirable than fossil fuels.

The market, however, is incapable of ensuring that the new energy supplies will displace fossil-fuel supplies joule for joule. In fact, history says that new energy sources typically add to the total energy pool rather than replacing it. The discovery of petroleum in the nineteenth century did not curb the killing of whales for their oil; in fact, the rate of killing increased thanks to the greater efficiency of oil-powered ships. The use of coal continued to rise throughout the era when oil became dominant; oil consumption kept rising after natural gas took off; and the burning of oil and gas has continued to increase despite growth in solar and wind generation.[192] Between 2009 and 2018, during a historically rapid buildup of U.S. wind and solar capacity, only one-fourth of the new output displaced electricity from fossil-fuel power plants; the other three-fourths went into increasing the total supply.[193]

Leaving the climate crisis up to technology improvement and business initiative is not going to deliver a winning strategy. In a 2019 article in the journal *Energy Research & Social Science*, Richard York and Shannon Elizabeth Bell put it this way: "The historical pattern of energy additions without energy transitions suggests that simply promoting renewables will not lead to a full transition. What is necessary is an active suppression of fossil fuels. Simply expanding renewables is unlikely to be effective, since, all else equal, adding more energy to the energy supply suppresses prices and, therefore, helps to spur consumption."[194]

Petroleum use in the United States escalated right through the Obama-era renewable energy boom, at a rate of 1.3 percent per year from 2012 to 2018. As always, a variety of factors economy-wide were involved. For example, because pickup trucks use about one-third more fuel per mile than do passenger cars, their soaring popularity has helped push U.S. gas and diesel consumption higher. And with ever-increasing numbers of air passengers and flights per year, commercial airlines are burning more fuel than ever. The oft-predicted national decline in use of fossil fuels is nowhere to be seen, and it is unlikely to occur on its own, at least until the next economic meltdown.[195]

There is a reason why new sources of energy don't completely replace old sources but instead add to existing supply. Growing economies need a growing pool of energy on which to draw, because, historically, increasing GDP is almost always accompanied by increased energy demand and, given that the current energy supply is heavy on fossil fuels, increased greenhouse emissions. Climate optimists have been predicting for years that economic growth will become "decoupled" from energy and material consumption. They foresee economies growing without limit while resource requirements and negative environmental impacts such as greenhouse emissions decline year by year. This prospect, known as "absolute decoupling,"[196] is the ecomodernists' central claim, and since 2015, decoupling has even been built into United Nations development goals. In both contexts, absolute decoupling serves as a fantasy through which policymakers can pretend that there are no inherent trade-offs among meeting basic human needs, environmental sustainability, and profit-making.[197] Back in the real world, however, no evidence of absolute decoupling has emerged.

For example, York and his colleague Julius McGee compiled data from 128 countries between 1960 and 2012, including per-capita GDP, the percentage of renewable energy derived from renewable sources, and carbon emissions. As usual, emissions and GDP were linked, rising or falling in concert over time. With a one-percent increase in per-capita GDP, per-capita emissions increased by an average of one-half percent. Surprisingly, the greater the share occupied by renewable sources in a nation's energy supply, the tighter the link between growth and carbon emissions. And in more affluent countries, increasing the renewable share was much less effective in reducing emissions than it was in less affluent countries. That's because in the richer nations, most new renewable capacity added to the energy supply; when it did displace another source, it was more often nuclear than fossil-fuel capacity that was taken down. "This suggests," York and McGee concluded, "that working to *deploy renewable energy* sources in developing nations may be a particularly important part of mitigating climate change, while trying to *reduce overall electricity consumption* in affluent nations is needed." (Emphasis added.)[198]

By importing large quantities of consumer goods rather than producing them in factories of their own, affluent countries have at times inadvertently created the illusion of absolute decoupling—appearing to have grown their economies while reducing emissions. In reality, they had merely "exported" a portion of their greenhouse emissions burden to developing countries. In July 2019, the European Environmental Bureau (EEB), a network of citizens' organizations spanning thirty nations, published a report examining the evidence for when and where GDP may have been decoupled from resource use and greenhouse emissions. Having amassed the results of more than 250 published studies, the Bureau report's authors found a few cases here and there in which emissions decreased as GDP rose. But all such cases were narrow, covering only a limited time span of one to a few years, or only a small geographic area. When emissions were found to have fallen alongside a rising GDP in a single country or region, it always turned out that only the emissions generated within that country's or region's borders had been counted; when the analysts also considered emissions produced elsewhere to manufacture goods that the country had imported, all evidence of decoupling disappeared.[199] And as the world's economies grow larger, decoupling will drift even further out of reach.[200] Not only are the limits to growth real, we've already overshot the limit for use of fossil fuels.

CONSERVATION IS PRICELESS

This is a good point at which to stress that the chief goal of climate action over the next decade will be, or at least should be, to reduce greenhouse emissions as rapidly as can be done humanely, fairly, and while restricting other kinds of ecological damage. A quick phase-out of fossil fuels, accompanied by a buildup of non-fossil energy capacity, will be mandatory; however, the renewable buildup will not be the force that drives down emissions. As experience has shown, simply introducing more wind and solar energy and more energy-efficient technologies into the market won't chase fossil fuels out. The new energy sources will have one purpose only: to partially fill the energy hole left by the forced exit of oil, gas, and coal. The statutory phaseout of fossil fuels will stimulate demand for renewables; the conversion won't happen the other way around.

There has long been broad support in the climate movement for reducing fossil fuel use by putting a price on carbon. The mechanism might be a carbon tax or, as in the European Union Emissions Trading System, a requirement that companies buy permits before they can sell dirty energy. The key question is how high the price of carbon will have to rise in order to reduce emissions at a sufficiently rapid pace. If, for example, the price of gasoline rises by 10 percent, we know that consumption won't automatically drop by 10 percent. So how far would a carbon tax have to rise in order to suppress consumption sufficiently?

Studies worldwide show that what economists call the "price elasticity" of energy consumption varies widely, but on average, a 10 percent rise in price (including taxes) results in no more than a 2 percent decrease in consumption.[201] So if we want a tax to push down consumption by 10 percent, it would need to add 50 percent to the cost of the fuel or electricity. If gasoline is selling at $2.50 per gallon, and given that each $1.00 per ton of carbon tax increases the price of gasoline by a penny, a tax of $125 per ton of carbon would be required to reduce consumption by even a meager 10 percent—in theory. You'd have to go ahead and impose the tax to learn what really happens.

Models employed by the Nobel Memorial Prize–winning economist William Nordhaus predicted in 2016 that to hold the global mean temperature rise down to even 2.5°C would require a carbon price of $230 per ton, rising to $350 in 2030 and to more than $1,000 in 2050.[202] Such prices could result in a politically noxious $12.50-per-gallon gas cost in today's money, and by allowing 2.5° of warming, they would still fail to prevent a climate crash. To keep warming down to 1.5°, which is widely considered to be the maximum safe rise, would require astronomical prices. For example, the IPCC's October 2018 report estimated that a carbon tax would need to rise as high as $27,000 per ton by 2100 to maintain 1.5°C. Compared with what would be required to stop greenhouse warming at a safe temperature, prices in today's carbon markets are comically small: $6 in the European system and $3 for Japan's carbon tax.

Nordhaus wrote that the action necessary to trigger a decline in emissions that could achieve even the weak 2.5° goal would "strain credulity." He saw no way to take such action, because he was operating within the bounds of the economics profession, where the kind of restraint needed to keep the Earth habitable for humans and other species is deemed, in his words, "unrealistically ambitious." If any system can guarantee the necessary emissions reductions, it will be one that places no trust in carbon pricing or the market in general but goes right to the bottom line of directly phasing out fossil fuels. Boston College sociologist Juliet Schor told me, "I've long believed that we need controls on energy demand; we can't do it only on the supply side. But I'm afraid we're past the point where we can do it with a price on carbon without major disruption. The price will go too high. Instead, it's going to take a lot of government intervention."[203]

James Boyce, a University of Massachusetts emeritus professor, believes that there is a way for a carbon price to succeed. As an example of what he envisions, let's say that each year, a national 1.5C-degree CO_2 emissions quota is established, and a corresponding number of permits are auctioned off to coal, oil, and gas suppliers. Companies will be required to hand over a dollar-value worth of permits corresponding to the carbon content of their product, writes Boyce, when they introduce it into the economy at the "ports, pipeline terminals, and mine heads." The total quantity of permits auctioned off would decline year by year, directly decreasing the annual amount of CO_2 emitted from fossil fuels.[204]

The system would have consequences for consumers. With a climate emergency already in progress, the clampdown on fossil energy would need to be imposed ASAP, even as development of new energy capacity remains in its infancy. With supply shrinking and demand still high and rising, the permit price would probably be bid up beyond any price predictable by the usual economic models. When energy prices rise, the prices of lots of other things rise. Recognizing that the inflation burden would fall hardest on low-income households, Boyce suggests that the entire amount of revenue collected in the dirty-energy auction be rebated to the public in equal per-person shares. That, he shows, would make the net economic impact highly progressive. With a carbon price of $200, households in the bottom 80 percent of the income scale would receive more from the rebate than they paid in higher prices, with the bottom 20 percent benefiting the most. The top 20 percent would pay out more in carbon tax than they receive from the rebate.

Boyce's plan to issue permits for a declining quantity of fossil fuels going into the system would be enough to achieve the required emissions reductions. The auction's only function, then, would be to determine who gets the permits. But rather than awarding permits to the companies with the deepest pockets and letting them allocate the limited quantities of fuels among their customers, why not distribute energy in a way that steers resources where they're needed for the public good?[205]

Although a system of auctions and rebates would benefit low-income, low-emissions households, there are better ways to do that. For example, the Green New Deal has a good approach, taking the gloves off labor to open up a fair fight over workers' rights while, as stated in the GND resolution, "providing all people of the United States with high-quality health care; affordable, safe, and adequate housing; economic security; and access to clean water, clean air, healthy and affordable food, and nature."

Carbon pricing—in effect, rationing by ability to pay—is also blind to what people are paying *for*. That is, every pound of CO_2 has the same dollar value at any given time, whether it constitutes "subsistence emissions" (to, say, heat one's home) or "luxury emissions" (to, say, fly to Aruba).[206] Thus, such an approach favors serving the rich few rather than serving the needs of the many. Punishment for either type of emissions is the same. Pricing also rewards every emission reduction equally, whether it comes from a short-term fix such as capturing a coal- or gas-fired power plant's emissions or a deeper effort with long-term impact, such as construction for passive solar heating or downdraft ventilation that could eliminate the need for air-conditioning.[207]

Carbon pricing has another thing going against it: Wherever it has been tried, it has been found politically toxic. In a 2014 issue of the journal *Carbon Management*, British analysts Shaun Chamberlin, Larch Maxey, and Victoria Hurth discussed the different impacts of "price-based" and "quantity-based" approaches to reducing emissions. The pricing approach is always found to be deeply unpopular. The government that enforces a price, and therefore a high energy cost, is rightly viewed as pitting all against all in an inequitable struggle to get enough of what we all need. Rebates don't buy back much good feeling, either. Chamberlin and colleagues argue that we instead need a system that fosters a sense that we're all in this together, and with a common purpose. They cite U.K.-focused surveys in which a hypothetical declining cap on fossil-fuel emissions backed up by an allocation of energy ration credits—everyone getting the same number of credits—received far higher approval than any of the price-based approaches. That is consistent with the spirit of solidarity that was exhibited by the U.K. and U.S. populations under rationing during World War II, and with a host of academic studies concluding that most people never act like the robotic utility-maximizing agents depicted in economic textbooks; rather, most humans value fairness above all.[208]

CUT OFF THEIR POWER

In late 2019, the United Nations issued its Production Gap Report, which came to a frightening conclusion regarding global fossil fuel use: "Governments are planning to produce about 50% more fossil fuels by 2030 than would be consistent with a 2°C [of warming] pathway and 120% more than would be consistent with a 1.5°C pathway."[209] The report's graphs show fossil-fuel use rising at a rate that would take the world beyond 3° of warming. It found that only a small handful of countries were making explicit efforts to reduce the use of oil, gas, and coal.

Given this situation, Richard York believes it's time for system change: "We inaccurately frame climate as a technical problem, when the problem lies in the structure of the economy and society. The solutions will have to be political and economic, not only technical. But a politician can't run a campaign on that." He adds, "This is a blunt point, but it must be made: we must directly suppress fossil fuels. It will require strong regulation to prevent extraction."[210]

Today, the United States is one of the countries hurtling in the opposite direction, with increasing fossil fuel extraction and use. The nongovernmental organization Global Energy Monitor reported in 2019 that more than 150 new oil and gas pipelines were under development in North America, and that once they're completed, the product they deliver will dump 560 million metric tons of CO_2 into the atmosphere annually.[211] That would amount to more than a 10 percent increase in U.S. emissions at the very moment that such contaminants need to be decreasing by as much as 10 percent per year. The most active area for new pipeline capacity was the Permian Basin of West Texas, a supersize, twenty-first-century version of those 1950s Hollywood oil gushers. Since 2014, the 75,000-square-mile region has increased its oil and gas output by the energy equivalent of 4 million barrels of oil per day—nine times the nation's total solar energy output and three times the wind output. And that's just the *increase* in fossil-fuel extraction in one part of a single U.S. state.

Ted Nace, a co-author of the report, told *The Guardian*, "These pipelines are a bet that the world won't get serious about climate change, allowing the incumbency of oil and gas to strengthen."[212] That will remain a safe bet as long as there is no direct suppression of oil, gas, and coal extraction, along with a dismantling of power plants and other fossil-fuel infrastructure.

The first step toward the abolition of fossil fuels should be to stop encouraging them. The federal and state governments hand over about $20 billion worth of subsidies to the fossil-fuel industry each year. According to the nonprofit Oil Change International, "A particularly important subset are subsidies for exploration, which incentivize expanding fossil fuel reserves, including the discovery of new resources. Production subsidies also include support for access, appraisal, development, extraction, preparation, transport (to utilities and refineries), plant construction and operation (of utilities and refineries), distribution (fuel products and fossil-fuel-based electricity) and decommissioning."[213] Those subsidies have to go, but much broader efforts will be required to end all extraction.

The federal government also has the power to kick the dirty-energy business off public land. The Keep It in the Ground Act of 2015, which would end new oil, coal, and gas leases, has floundered for years in Congress. Several contenders for the 2020 Democratic presidential nomination called for banning new leases on federal lands or seabeds for oil and gas exploration and drilling.[214] But if restrictions were to stop there, the fuels extracted from federal lands already under lease would continue to flow into the economy, as would all fuels coming off private lands—the latter responsible for three-fourths of U.S. carbon emissions from oil and gas.[215]

Governments can and should adopt other so-called supply-side policies to reduce the quantity of fossil fuels entering the economy: a nationwide ban on oil and gas drilling on private lands; a moratorium on construction of oil and gas terminals, pipelines, and refineries; and prohibitions on specific extraction methods such as hydraulic fracturing, tar-sand mining, and strip mining.[216]

For the government, supply-side suppression of fossil fuels has political advantages over such mechanisms as carbon taxes. Targeting the never-popular oil, gas, and coal companies gets broader support than targeting invisible CO_2 molecules. Regulatory action is perceived as fairer and less burdensome than taxes (in this case, by everyone except the fossil fuel companies).[217] However, none of these indirect policies could ensure that necessarily deep, year-by-year emissions reductions would be achieved. To do that, York and others believe, the government may need to play its ace: nationalization of the fossil fuel industries.[218]

Public pressure has also been brought to bear on the dirty-energy companies from outside the government. Although the Obama-era pipeline struggles did not succeed in stopping the flow of oil, they did raise the moral stakes of the fight against the fossil fuel giants. Then there's the grassroots movement known as Keep It in the Ground, which aims at ending all mining and drilling on both public and private lands. Under its banner in 2015, 400 civil society organizations in more than sixty countries called on "world leaders to put an immediate halt to new fossil fuel development and pursue a just transition to renewable energy with a managed decline of the fossil fuel industry." In a nice punch line to their statement, the groups alluded to the old adage about what to do if you've dug yourself into a hole: "The first step in this effort is a simple one: Stop digging."[219] The campaign has made an excellent case for keeping fossil fuels in the ground, but it has not articulated a plan for making that happen.

Since 2011, a fossil fuel divestment movement has been calling for institutional investors to shed all of their stock in coal, oil, and gas companies. In its first three years, the divestment movement won over more than 250 universities, cities and counties, pension funds, foundations, and faith-based organizations. Significantly, many of the larger institutions that divested were located outside the United States.[220] At the end of 2018, Bill McKibben and 350.org, who have been out front on divestment since 2012, announced that more 1,000 institutions, with over $8 trillion in assets collectively, had committed to divestment. By that time, the total sum disinvested from coal companies amounted to more than 10 percent of the total market value of all coal stocks.[221]

With the coal industry already in decline, some of the major disinvestment announcements were followed by drops in prices of coal shares, but the majority of such events had no apparent effect. Disinvestment amounted to only a fraction of one percent of oil and gas companies' total market value, and it did not have a significant effect on their share prices.[222] However, disinvestment is not aimed first and foremost at squeezing companies financially. Julie Ayling and Neil Gunningham of Australian National University write, "Although [the global disinvestment movement] argues that institutional investors should divest fossil fuel shareholdings, it is under few illusions about the prospect of success, and it is well aware that others are likely to purchase divested stocks. Its primary role is . . . concerned with labeling a particular behavior (carbon pollution) as morally reprehensible, and, by so doing, shifting attitudes about climate change mitigation."[223]

The market isn't going to flush fossil energy out of the economy, even if oil, gas, and coal are made a lot more costly through a carbon price. Ending subsidies, locking companies out of public lands, banning fracking, busting pipelines, stopping oil and gas exports, and depriving dirty-fuel companies of investment are now necessary. But even all of those actions taken together will not be enough to drive fossil fuel burning down to zero in time. More is needed.

Calling for a "human needs approach" to the climate emergency, Moriarty and Honnery write, "We conclude that we must actively plan for a future in which emissions of CO_2 are reduced by minimization of energy use—a low-energy future. Because present growth-oriented economies will be incapable of making timely reductions in emissions, we argue that a new approach emphasizing social change is needed to achieve this, one in which provision of basic human needs replaces economic growth as the focus for economic activity."[224]

The two scholars came to that insight because they'd been asking the right questions. Given humanity's and the Earth's predicament, too many others are asking much less relevant ones. Cornucopian researchers are asking, "How much more renewable energy can we produce if we repeal Murphy's Law and everything goes as we hope it will?" Energy companies and their investors are asking, "What's going to bring the biggest return?" Economists are asking, "What is going to optimize the global cost-benefit ratio between now and 2100?" Politicians and candidates are asking, "How far out front can I go on climate without scaring away votes?" And think tanks are asking, "What will fly in the House and Senate?" The political struggle is indeed crucial, but it can easily get sidetracked into half-measures unless we keep asking, at every step along the way, the most important question of all: "What is now ecologically and morally necessary?"

It is now necessary to do three things simultaneously: drive emissions down to zero; adapt society to a smaller energy supply while still producing as much non-fossil energy as is required for sustenance and good quality of life; and ensure fair, equitable access to resources and economic security. At the same time, goals of social and economic justice such as those envisioned in the Green New Deal must be made reality. Any comprehensive strategy to prevent climate catastrophe must be judged on whether it can meet all of those standards. The Green New Deal is an important step in the right direction, but it alone will not steer us clear of the hot abyss. We need a strategy that includes a Green New Deal while going beyond it.

The current absence of such a strategy then raises one more question: If we set out to do what is necessary, how will that journey unfold, and what kind of country do we need to become?

4

❦

OFF-RAMP AHEAD

"Science shows we have barely 10 years to avoid disaster, suggesting we shouldn't count entirely on technological innovation or self-moderation. Meanwhile, we're all in a lifeboat with just enough space for each of us. Should we really be complaining about not getting first-class seats if doing so would bump others?"

—Eleanor Boyle, 2019[225]

Someday—and it had better be soon—Americans will mobilize to prevent the ecological catastrophe that is being forecast by scientists. Despite the overwhelming evidence that immediate action is demanded, most people in this country don't seem prepared to do that yet. Politicians and pro-corporate economists are stuck in an endless loop, rejecting ideas for climate action because of their potential short-term impact on profit instead of their long-term capacity to create a stable, sustainable, and just society. We can't limit the array of actions under consideration to those that appear to be politically and economically achievable under current conditions. If it turns out that existing institutions are unable to accept or support the policies and actions that are essential to addressing ecological meltdown, then it is those institutions, not the necessary actions, that need to be overhauled.

The U.S. economy will always be recalcitrant to any form of restraint, but political acceptability is a moving target. The past few years' climate news alone has demonstrated the whiplash speed with which public consciousness can shift. The growing awareness now has to be expanded dramatically, and that will require a blunt, forthright discussion of how profoundly our nation is going to have to change in the hot and increasingly unstable decades ahead.

GOING ON AN ENERGY DIET

If fossil fuels are rapidly eliminated during the transition to non-fossil energy, the pool of energy available to society will shrink. How much it shrinks will depend on how fast the new energy capacity and a new electric grid can be developed. And if the transition succeeds, the handy liquid fuels that for a century have powered road travel, farming, freight hauling, and air travel will be flushed out of society forever. Operating buildings, transportation, and industry mostly on electricity will be much more complicated. But adapting to a leaner energy diet does not have to be a grim ordeal; in fact, it will provide opportunities to scale back the environmental and societal damage that potent, portable energy sources, especially liquid fuels, have empowered us to inflict.

The United States can reduce its energy consumption by first starving the harmful and wasteful parts of the economy that should have been curtailed already on other grounds. The cutting can start in the U.S. military, which produces more greenhouse emissions than most entire countries do—a huge quantity of it from jet fuel.[226] The cuts should extend to demilitarizing law enforcement and abolishing mass incarceration. We can slash the energy allowance of the nation's most affluent people, who account for a disproportionate share of energy consumption and emissions; by one estimate, households having more than $1 million in investment assets are contaminating the Earth's atmosphere with ten times more greenhouse emissions than the average household.[227] Cutting harm and waste can get us some distance toward eliminating emissions, but it won't be enough. A lower-energy economy will need to produce fewer goods and services overall—still enough necessary products to go around, just less production of goods that contribute little more than profits to the seller and waste to the landfill.

Living with lower energy consumption doesn't have to mean a life of deprivation and hardship. On this point, some international comparisons may be useful. Let's say we cut this country's total energy consumption in half. Today, five countries consume approximately half as much energy per capita as the United States does: Denmark, Japan, Slovakia, Slovenia, and Switzerland.[228] All are well-functioning societies with good quality of life. And, according to the United Nations, they all rank higher on the Human Development Index scale than the United States does.[229]

Looking lower down the energy scale, where countries consume about one-fourth as much energy per capita as we do, we find Argentina, Croatia, Cyprus, and Romania. These countries rank slightly lower in Human Development Index than the United States, but all are within the U.N.'s "High" or "Very High" categories. Some of these countries would clearly be better places to live than others, but the larger point is that consuming 75 percent less energy per person than the United States doesn't require a society to adopt a monastic lifestyle.

Shrinking energy use will shrink production of goods and services, and therefore wealth production. A smaller economy would not necessarily be a bad thing. Decades of research have shown that once GDP per person is sufficient to ensure security in food, housing, medical care, education, and other necessities, further increases in GDP do not bring an enduring improvement in people's life satisfaction.[230] Accordingly, bringing America's bloated GDP down to size and curing the economy's cruelly high level of inequality will improve the quality of life for millions of Americans and make us a better society. To reach that goal, we have a long way to go. Jason Hickel has formulated a Sustainable Development Index that incorporates elements of the Human Development Index but penalizes high per-capita material consumption. When Hickel ranked most of the world's nations by their Sustainable Development Index, the United States came in at fifth from the bottom, at number 159.[231]

When it's pumping up elite lifestyles, renewable energy is not green energy. Hickel makes a convincing case that "reducing inequality needs to be at the very heart of climate policy."[232] A less unequal society will also be a happier society overall. The purpose of consumption is supposedly to satisfy needs and make us happy, but our brains evaluate the satisfaction we derive from our own consumption by comparing it with the consumption of those around us. An increase in the income or wealth of our friends and neighbors makes us feel less affluent ourselves; on the other hand, seeing those around us build better social relationships makes us more, not less, satisfied with our own personal networks.[233]

Don Fitz has painted an encouraging picture of a society living with less energy and less production. A society that has stopped investing labor and energy in mass incarceration and militarism, he says, will be more humane. Walkable, livable communities will be free of private-vehicle traffic; air, noise, and light pollution; and other dangers. A transformed food system will ensure better nutrition for all. Free neighborhood public and community clinics will provide preventive medical care, reducing by several sizes the economic and environmental footprint of today's profit-driven medical industries. "The concept of changing consciousness is empty if we are forced to participate in harmful production with no power to curb it," Fitz writes. "Every group of working people needs to ask if what they are producing is good or harmful. Should it be increased, changed, reduced or abolished? If they decide that what they produce needs to be reduced or halted, how should the changes be made and what alternative jobs should they have?"[234]

TO SHARE THE WEALTH, SHARE THE WORK

Overproducing for the sake of wealth accumulation rather than human fulfillment, the world's big economies are hurtling along a highway to ecological ruin and had better start looking for an exit ramp. In the 1960s, *Monopoly Capital* showed that modern economies tend to stagnate because of overproduction, an overaccumulation of surplus, and a lack of lucrative ways to invest it. In the 1970s, *The Limits to Growth* showed how overproduction would lead, inevitably, to collapse—not just economic decline but a civilizational crash. Together they tell us that eliminating the surplus by reducing production will help prevent that crash and, in the process, tame energy consumption, reduce ecological damage, and end the exploitation of working people. If production is to be reduced, that surplus output can be cut back, paving the way for a shorter workweek with full pay.

Payrolls usually make up the bulk of employers' costs, so sub-stituting technology, and the energy it consumes, for human power whenever possible is a time-proven way to increase the surplus going to business owners. The resulting increases in labor productivity have boosted profits, but at the cost of accelerating the drive toward over-accumulation and stagnation. And higher productivity has not been rewarded with higher pay for workers,[235] so increased output per hour of work has been going almost entirely to enrich owners and top managers. Working people have not benefited from the growth of an economy in which they are laboring harder and longer. Giorgos Kallis, the author of the book *Degrowth*, explains why shorter working hours will be necessary:

> Without growth, unemployment increases because rising pro-ductivity reduces the amount of labor necessary. Work-sharing refers to a reduction of the hours of paid work without loss in income. Fewer working hours per person leave more jobs for everyone to share. . . . Work-sharing redistributes the gains from productivity. Instead of producing profits for capitalists, productivity serves to liberate time for workers. . . . [W]ork-sharing is a fundamental condition for a stable, zero-growth path in both neoclassical and Keynesian growth models. Econometric studies suggest that reduced working hours re-duce carbon emissions and environmental pressures and in-crease wellbeing. There is a limit, however, to how far work can be reduced. If the use of fossil fuels is to be limited in the future, there will be less "energy slaves" doing work for free. Humans will have to do more of this work—if we want to work less, then we will also have to be satisfied with less con-sumption. In a carbon- and oil-constrained world, automation and "robotization" are not inevitable outcomes.[236]

The New Economics Foundation has long advocated shorter hours for workers. It contends that a shorter workweek would have numerous positive effects beyond reducing emissions: lower unem-ployment; greater social and economic equality; less dependence on debt; more time for more fulfilling unpaid activities, including community endeavors; reduced stress, as we "move away from the current path of living to work, working to earn, and earning to consume"; reduced need for child care and more time to spend with one's children; more opportunity to enjoy and deepen relationships with family, friends, and neighbors; greater equality between women and men; "more equal shares of paid and unpaid work"; and "more time to participate in local activities, to find out what's going on around us, to engage in politics, locally and nationally, to ask questions and to campaign for change."[237]

Is it anti-capitalist to be anti-growth? Degrowth scholars and activists don't typically start with the ecosocialist principle that if humanity is to achieve an ecologically sustainable existence, capitalism has got to go. But most degrowthers also do not expect capitalism to survive if its unrestrained accumulation of surplus is choked off and the exploitation of the working people who produce that surplus is abolished;[238] after all, it's state-sanctioned accumulation and exploitation that define capitalism. Therefore, whether we set off on the journey calling for the end of growth or for the end of capitalism, we're checking our bags to the same final destination (preferably on a train).

What might a society look like when it prioritizes human well-being for all at the expense of growth for some? That question could be answered with a utopian vision, as long as we keep in mind Kallis's admonition that "There is a place for utopias, but utopia not as a blueprint but as a canvas." The visions that have given the word a bad reputation, he says, are ones like the free-market utopia: strictly prescriptive and demanding blind adherence to a particular story of how things should be. He argues that a degrowth utopia is "open, malleable, and plural" and can "open up our minds to a horizon of possibilities, which in turn shape our actions today."[239]

Ernest Callenbach's 1975 novel *Ecotopia* is consistent with Kallis's description, envisioning a degrowth society in concrete, plausible terms, complete with a twenty-hour workweek.[240] The novel is presented in the form of dispatches sent in 1999 by one William Weston, the first U.S. journalist to enter the northern Pacific Coast region after it had declared its independence from the United States in 1980 and become the nation of Ecotopia. One of the Ecotopian legislature's first acts was to pass a law decreeing a twenty-hour workweek. Writes Callenbach, "This would mean sacrifice of present consumption, but it would ensure future survival." This simple act would also trigger an economic revolution: "This philosophical change may have seemed innocent on the surface. Its grave implications were soon spelled out, however. Ecotopian economists . . . were well aware that the standard of living could only be sustained and increased by relentless pressure on work hours." However, "Ecotopian militants" put out the word that "economic disaster was not identical with survival disaster for persons," and that a financial contraction would push the nation to devote its "energy, knowledge, skills, and materials to the basic necessities of survival." In other words, let GDP fall hard; it consists largely of wasteful and luxury spending anyway. Big Business would flee back to the United States or elsewhere, and "most factories, farms, and other productive facilities would fall into Ecotopian hands like ripe plums."

Although he published the book more than a decade before climate change would become a global issue, Callenbach had the Ecotopians doing an awful lot of climate-friendly things for other, equally good reasons. Aircraft were barred from the national airspace. Dirty or harmful industries were shut down. As in the United States of the 1940s, the numbers of product types and brands were deeply reduced. Food waste was almost completely eliminated. Private automobiles were not manufactured within the country and were barred from all densely populated areas. Ecotopians got around within their capital city of San Francisco by hopping into "comical battery-driven contraptions" resembling the city's historically famous cable cars. These minibuses crept along at ten miles per hour but appeared at each stop every five minutes. Market Street had become a pedestrian mall featuring stony creeks and thousands of trees.[241] Callenbach even foresaw pick-up/drop-off bikes, but in Ecotopia they were ridden free of charge.

"Minicities"—each a cluster of wood-frame apartment buildings surrounding a workplace—were located along rail lines throughout Ecotopia. Much of the green infrastructure and parkland was created by public programs reminiscent of the New Deal's Works Progress Administration. The famous twenty-hour workweek was somewhat fluid. It was said of Ecotopia that "you often can't tell the difference between work and leisure." Many intellectuals were members of the "ordinary factory and farm workforce." But this was not a nation of Luddites; it was connected to the United States by a bullet train, and it sheepishly imported metals to build electric vehicles for export.

Callenbach had no romantic illusions about his fictional society; Weston, the reporter, chuckled over the Ecotopians' often corny habits, as when, rather than repairing their streets' potholes, they would turn them into flower beds. They objectified First Nations people as vessels of nature's wisdom ("Many Ecotopians are sentimental about Indians, and there's some sense in which they envy the Indians their lost natural place in the American wilderness"[242]), with seemingly no recognition that the Ecotopians and the U.S.-Americans before them were occupiers of First Nations' land. And then there's a well-meant but excruciatingly 1970s-ish, stereotype-filled three pages under the heading "Race in Ecotopia: Apartheid or Equality?"[243] Callenbach, who died in 2012, told the *New York Times* in 2008 that his purpose in those pages had been to reflect "Black nationalist ideas of the time," but his attempt bombs out badly these days.[244]

GETTING ACROSS THE STARTING LINE

Today, we can imagine with varying degrees of confidence some characteristics of a future society that has eliminated greenhouse emissions and deeply restored ecological stability. In that future society as in Ecotopia, private transportation and air travel would be rigorously curtailed and public transportation would be expanded and designed to serve people's needs. Housing would be affordable, functional, energy efficient, and of modest size, with more of it in multi-unit buildings. Residential areas would be located near public transportation lines and workplaces. Urban landscapes would have much less concrete and much more vegetation. Food would be produced in harmony with the ecosystem. Both production and waste would be reduced. And people would spend far less time on the job and more time with their families, friends, and communities.

The way to create a lower-energy society is not simply to do as the Croatians or Romanians do. For the most part, the countries that are living today on more modest energy expenditure than we do—that is, almost all countries—didn't shrink but rather grew into their current degree of consumption. When reductions in energy demand have occurred, they usually were imposed by economic decline or collapse, as occurred in the Soviet Union of the 1990s. Much can be learned from Indigenous societies that have lived for extended periods in equilibrium with available resources, yet we are faced with a very different challenge: to voluntarily reduce our excessive rate of energy consumption to a sustainable rate. If we manage to scale back intentionally and significantly while at the same time ensuring sufficiency for all and improving quality of life, we will have performed a feat that is historically unprecedented for any large nation. Like all great feats, it will require preparation and training. Before getting into the details of what the shift to a sustainable energy diet will require at the national scale, let's consider how individuals, households, and communities can prepare now for the transformation.

There is broad agreement on the actions that we can take as individuals. Curtailing use of cars and trucks and increasing use of public transportation will reduce the burning of fossil fuels and allow a more sustainable redesign of cities and suburbs. Living in a small, well-insulated home and as close to work as is feasible will further those goals. Eating no meat or at least no meat from feedlots or confinement operations will help reduce greenhouse emissions, soil degradation, water contamination, and human health problems; growing one's own food in home or community gardens will help achieve those same goals. By avoiding air travel, we can help curtail one of the most rapidly growing and dangerous sources of greenhouse gases. Installing home or community solar electric capacity and solar water heating can further reduce fossil-fuel use, *if* the money thus saved does not go to support greater consumption elsewhere in the marketplace. And perhaps the easiest adjustment to make is simply to buy a lot less stuff. Notice that doing all those things closely reflects what would be an everyday necessity not just in a green utopian novel but in any realistic vision of a sustainable society capable of sticking around for the long haul.

System change is essential; voluntary personal change is helpful along the way. For many people in the United States, taking every possible step that we should take will be difficult. Some actions will initially be unaffordable to many. Others will require major changes in the built environment and living arrangements. Sometimes it's not easy to take such big steps when a quick look around tells you few others are doing it. Therefore, in addition to doing our own part as much as we can, it is important to support collective efforts that, if successful, will make it easier for everyone to do what is necessary to live in a sustainable and ecologically stable society.

A debate has raged for years over the impact of individual lifestyle change versus system change. Environmental writer Sami Grover has called for an end to the argument over which is more important to tackle first, contending that we should try to do both:

> Even the most vocal proponent of personal lifestyle change is not doing all they can. Conversely, even the most adamant adherent of the "systemic change is all that matters" argument is, most likely, still taking steps to limit their footprint. In other words, most of us are doing something, and none of us are doing enough. And that's perfectly OK. The goal is not—as Big Oil would gladly have us believe—to "save the world" one bike ride, or one veggie burger, at a time. But rather, it is to use personal lifestyle change as a lever to push for broader, society-wide change.[245]

Grover gives a striking example: "When we ride our bikes, our power lies not in cutting our personal travel footprint—an impact that seems trivial when surrounded by gigantic, diesel-chugging trucks. Instead, it's in creating a space where politicians and planners feel confident investing in bike-friendly infrastructure and policies. Just visit Copenhagen or Amsterdam and compare their streets today to car-clogged photos from the Sixties." Cycling and activism, reinforcing each other, have helped reduce greenhouse emissions in both cities. Grover's advice is to take action to reduce your personal footprint, but don't talk about it much. If opportunities arise to leverage personal actions in furtherance of broader efforts, take them. Simply lecturing others to "do as I do" will always be self-defeating. On that, he quotes leading climate scientist-activist Michael Mann's response to a critic: "My followers know (1) I don't eat meat out of choice, (2) I don't believe in dictating to others what they should eat & that, furthermore (3) doing so would almost certainly backfire & be counterproductive to efforts to engage the public more broadly on climate action."[246]

Joseph Nevins, an author and professor of geography at Vassar College, maintains that individual and collective efforts are not just complementary; they are necessarily interdependent. To illustrate, he asks us to imagine a person who routinely engages in racist behavior, and who, when people condemn him for it, "argues that a focus on his actions is foolhardy and that he, as a true anti-racist, dedicates his energies to fighting structural racism." Such a person, Nevins notes, would not be taken seriously. The fact that people often do accept this degree of personal hypocrisy with regard to climate and other "environmental" issues, he argues, "reflects how they imagine nature: as outside of social power and not involving dynamic ties between structures and individual agency."[247]

I have not been especially diligent about climate in my personal life, but I believe there are important reasons why I should, especially if it's done in the strategic ways that Grover advocates. Using fewer resources expresses solidarity with people in the global South, where climate change hits first and hardest and access to resources is limited. Weaning ourselves off high levels of energy use now is good practice for a future in which a weaning is going to happen, like it or not. Now is the time to move to the opposite pole from the ecomodernists, toward a *closer* relationship with nature. Writing for *Resilience*, Wes Jackson and Robert Jensen made this case eloquently:

> Ecosystems are far more creative than human systems. Consider a modern city, the product of the human-generated information used to build the housing, businesses, infrastructure, and transportation networks that allow millions to live in close quarters, often with exciting results (both constructive and destructive). All that excitement leads us to ignore the fact that

these cities of the industrial age are made possible only through massive expenditures of fossil energy and other resources, some of which come from the other side of the planet. Meanwhile, natural ecosystems are home to a much more expansive variety of creatures living in far more complex relationships, requiring none of that fossil energy to maintain. Natural ecosystems can maintain themselves for countless millennia using only solar flows, while cities draw down millions of years of concentrated energy in a relative blink of an eye. Which model provides a standard for our future?[248]

The climate movement has a strong moral foundation, which should not get lost in the rush to build a new society; otherwise, the future could end up as unequal and exploitative as the present, only fed by different energy sources. The climate argument can't be made solely on the basis of morality, however. Ample evidence shows that when people voluntarily act in a way that they perceive as morally correct, they are more likely to engage later in selfish or otherwise immoral behavior. Psychologists attribute this tendency to a common but unstated belief that "good" actions or even thoughts provide us with a degree of "moral license." The phenomenon has been characterized as a "moral bank account" into which we deposit good deeds and withdraw moral currency. With energy conversion, the problem of moral license seems to affect not only individuals but also society as a whole. When fossil fuels are the dominant energy source, environmentally conscious communities may stress conservation measures, block reckless developers, and restrict the use of private cars. With growing availability of "clean" wind and solar power and increased sales of electric cars, however, regulators could feel morally licensed to approve new, resource-hungry development of all kinds, tolerate increased vehicle traffic, and allow programs for home insulation or other conservation to lapse.[249] Moral arguments for either personal or collective ecological action have to be accompanied by arguments based on global necessity.

Personal climate action can be expressed not only through reducing our own consumption but also through greater civic involvement:

going regularly to meetings of the city council or local planning board; pushing for community wind and solar power; or urging the organizations we belong to or contribute to, the schools or universities we attend or work for, and all other employers to dump any investments they may have in fossil fuels or other dirty industries. We can also call on friends and neighbors to urge their city or county government to join the thousand others who have passed climate emergency resolutions. The existing resolutions consist of strong official declarations that there is a climate emergency, with no hard commitment to act immediately. They are intended, however, to be followed up with action. Cities from Boulder, Colorado, to Darebin, Australia, have done that by pursuing Climate Emergency Action Plans. Even Los Angeles, longtime mascot for America's disregard of ecological reality, now has a Climate Emergency Mobilization Office to lead the city's efforts.[250]

Any of us with time and means available can get involved in nationwide efforts, by helping get out the vote to elect candidates at all levels of government who will commit to supporting the Green New Deal's just transition and an airtight, declining cap on all fossil fuels; helping maintain relentless pressure on members of Congress to pass such legislation, with ten times as much vigor as we showed in defending ObamaCare in 2017; becoming involved in emerging "blue-green" alliances between the labor and climate movements; and joining strategic boycott movements (imagine the impact of audacious mass boycotts of air travel, or house and car buying).

More mass actions are coming. They will extend and transcend the potent movements of recent years: Occupy, Extinction Rebellion, Poor People's Campaign, Standing Rock, Sunrise, and Climate Strikes. We all have to get out there to defend the Earth. In a September 2019 commentary titled, "Scientists Must Act On Our Own Warnings to Humanity," Charlie Gardner and Claire Wordley of the University of Kent wrote that professionals such as scientists are not exempt:

> As conservation scientists and members of Extinction Rebellion, we encourage our fellow scientists to join us in embracing activism. In April 2019, over 12,000 scientists signed a letter endorsing the global school strikes, which are acts of civil

disobedience, and praising the movement as "justified and supported by the best available science." We ask that scientists take this one step further, and themselves join civil disobedience movements.[251]

Even with widespread and vigorous personal, civil-society, local, regional, and statewide climate efforts, fully eliminating America's greenhouse emissions will require federal regulation and coordination. Smaller communities of people function better than larger ones, but eliminating the greenhouse emissions of an entire economy comprising 330 million people cannot be accomplished one community or one state at a time. It would be a big mistake if, in order to green itself, a state or region tried to secede from the Union as the fictional Ecotopia did, or as the Yes California Independence Campaign has urged.[252] Getting control of our recklessly outsize national emissions will be difficult enough; the exit of a large, more ecologically conscious population would only strengthen the pro-fossil-fuel forces in the rest of the country.

CAP AND COPE

The Green New Deal resolution introduced in the House and Senate calls for rapid reductions in greenhouse emissions but does not say how we will eliminate the fossil fuels that produce them. A follow-up resolution for a climate emergency introduced by Sanders, Ocasio-Cortez, and Rep. Earl Blumenauer (D-Ore.) a few months later (see Appendix 2) calls for a "managed phase-out of the use of oil, gas, and coal to keep fossil fuels in the ground," but does not specify a mechanism for doing so.[253] Both were resolutions only, so even if they could have been passed in the face of a Republican-controlled Senate, neither would have authorized or funded any action by the government. But what if there comes a political opening to combine legislation creating a just transition to a renewable-energy economy with legislation mandating a surefire, rapid elimination of oil, gas, and coal use? What policies would that legislation need to contain, at minimum, if we're finally to get ourselves on the road to stopping the Earth's warming before it's too late?

I'm now going to take a stab at answering those questions. To keep up with the emission-reduction schedules set by the IPCC and the United Nations' 2019 Emissions Gap Report, implementing the Green New Deal will require a hard, declining limit on fossil-fuel extraction and use. In 2019, Larry Edwards and I proposed a direct, sure-fire mechanism for ratcheting down the extraction and combustion of oil, gas, and coal, by law and on schedule, simultaneous with non-fossil energy development and a just transition.[254] Drawing on portions of that plan, which we called "cap-and-adapt," along with other sources, I will now describe the steps that I believe are absolutely essential to prevent climate disaster.

The first, most crucial action will be to put an impervious cap on the nation's total supply of fossil fuel. The cap I'm talking about has nothing to do with the largely discredited cap-and-trade strategy that has been used in Europe and elsewhere. This cap is leakproof, with no waivers, workarounds, offsets, or any other gimmickry. It's really three caps: one each on oil, gas, and coal. Most importantly, it ratchets downward by a fixed amount year by year until it liberates us from fossil fuels entirely.

The simplest way to guarantee freedom from fossil fuels on schedule is with an annual mandatory reduction in the supply of each fuel. If the target is, say, to emancipate ourselves from fossil fuels within twenty years, then oil, natural gas, and coal extraction each will have to be reduced every year by 5 percent of the amount that was extracted in the year before the reduction begins. To do the job in ten years would require an annual reduction equal to 10 percent of the initial annual extraction. (The UN Emissions Gap Report would split the difference, calling for an annual 7.6 percent reduction in greenhouse emissions.)[255]

To enforce the cap, the government would issue permits each year to the companies that extract and sell fossil fuels. The permits would be denominated in terms of barrels of oil, cubic feet of gas, or tons of coal, not in carbon units or dollars. The total number of permits issued would reflect the total quantity of each class of fuel allowed into the system under that year's cap. No company or individual could pull any amount of fuel out of the ground without handing over the permits to cover that amount. To keep the cap hermetically sealed and the availability of fuels adequate, both imports and exports of all three fuels would be phased out. Similar systems for eliminating greenhouse gases other than carbon—for example, refrigerants—would also be required. (Further along, I'll discuss the reduction of greenhouse-gas emissions from agriculture and other land uses.)

We have seen that the carbon footprints of high-consumption countries are underestimated when large shares of the goods they consume are produced in foreign lands. That leaves millions of tons of manufacturing and farming emissions on the carbon accounts of the mostly lower-income "developing" countries where the goods are produced. Bernie Sanders's 2020 campaign climate plan took a step in the right direction by calling for a carbon fee on imported goods, but a fee would not guarantee rapid enough reductions. Instead, a direct system is needed to restrict import of goods whose production and shipping contribute to global warming. Each type of imported good would be classified according to the relative quantity of greenhouse gases released during its production and delivery. Permits would be auctioned off to shipping companies and other cargo haulers, who presumably would pass that cost back up the supply chain. The companies importing goods into the United States would surrender to customs agents a quantity of permits corresponding to their cargo's climate impact. A gradually declining cap would annually reduce the total number of permits, thus reducing the amount of greenhouse emissions released in connection with the consumption of imported products to zero by a specified deadline.

In the scenario that I have described, the leakproof fossil-fuel cap is the one national policy that is essential to driving down greenhouse emissions on schedule. The policies I suggest below, aimed at achieving sufficiency and a good life for all, are just that—suggestions. Call them a "cap and cope" plan.[256] Our society will have to adjust as the situation evolves. No one can predict how the coping will be accomplished in practice, but far-reaching measures must be agreed upon if an entire nation is to achieve fairness and sufficiency during the rapid elimination of climate-disrupting fuels. I am attempting here to navigate between the impossibly sunny forecasts of the energy cornucopians and the grim resignation of writers like *The Uninhabitable Earth*'s author David

Wallace Wells or the novelist Jonathan Franzen, who penned a notorious 2019 *New Yorker* piece titled "What If We Stopped Pretending the Climate Apocalypse Can Be Stopped?" In the article, Franzen declared that preventing ecological catastrophe is unachievable, based solely on climate "models" that he claimed to have run ten thousand times "through my brain." These cranial models told Franzen that effective action on greenhouse emissions is incompatible with "human nature," a term he used when he should have been using "capitalism."[257]

The angst that gripped the climate movement after the 2016 election began to proliferate rapidly throughout society with the alarming 2018 Intergovernmental Panel on Climate Change report. Mental health professionals and journalists have since been tracking the rise of what has come to be called "climate grief," loosely defined as "depression, anxiety, and mourning over climate change."[258] Climate grief continued to spread, accelerating further with the failure of the December 2019 Madrid climate talks to make any progress at all on curbing emissions. Robert Jensen, who has been writing about deep ecological grief, including his own, since well before 2016, says that such feelings are "exactly why we need to engage rather than avoid the distressing realities of our time. If we are afraid to speak honestly, we suffer alone. Better that we tell the truth and accept the consequences, together."[259]

In late 2019, *New York Times* columnist Michelle Goldberg wrote that climate grief has been joined by another pervasive phenomenon: "democracy grief." Along with its hostility toward any and all climate action, the Trump movement has proven, in her words, to be "pro-authoritarian and pro-oligarch. It has no interest in preserving pluralism, free and fair elections or any version of the rule of law that applies to the powerful as well as the powerless." Left to fester, wrote Goldberg, democracy grief (like climate grief) "can lead to apathy and withdrawal. Channeled properly, it can fuel an uprising." It is looking more and more as if a pro-authoritarian white minority—thirty-something percent of the population—could drag all of us, along with our nation's political system, past the point of no return. So if there is to be an uprising, it had better come soon. Goldberg concludes with a stern warning: "Democracy grief isn't like regular grief. Acceptance isn't how you move on from it. Acceptance is itself a kind of death."[260]

I am hopeful that both democracy grief and climate grief can be transformed into a hopeful and insurgent force capable of ridding us of their common source. Democratic structures are going to have to be rescued from the general drift toward authoritarianism before they can be strengthened in order to make effective federal action on climate possible. The defeat of Trumpism, however, will not automatically fling open the gates to either political sanity or ecological wholeness. The same powerful forces that have, in the name of corporate profit, blocked all efforts to achieve either political or climate justice will remain in place until they too can be overcome.

Given the dominating influence of such forces, freeing ourselves of fossil fuels on a tight schedule seems politically unrealistic, but that's no reason to surrender. Carrying on with business as usual will bring consequences too tragic to contemplate. And it's not a simple matter of action versus inaction, a coin flip with ecological stability on one side and the collapse of civilization on the other. The faster emissions can be reduced, the less dire the consequences. However, it is essential to adhere, come what may, to a clear goal: to break free of fossil fuels by the ecologically necessary deadline. My purpose here is to plant a flag and say this is how far the policies will have to go. Whenever someone floats more politically palatable proposals such as techno-fixes or carbon pricing that do not go far enough, I'll point ahead to that flag and remind them that speculative half-measures will not guarantee the required rate of emissions reduction. If, nevertheless, only half-measures are adopted, everyone should be fully aware that emissions are still going to overrun safe limits. And the further we overshoot those limits, the more unmanageable the consequences are going to be.

FAIR ENOUGH?

A leakproof, declining cap on fossil fuels is a necessary step to constrain global warming and stabilize the ecosphere,[261] but doing so will have huge economic repercussions, and it's hard to imagine Big Petroleum, Big Coal, or private utility companies going along with anything like it. As they have throughout their history, they will use their great wealth and pervasive influence in Washington to fight or sabotage this or any serious attempt to further regulate fossil fuels.[262] Therefore, I expect that a Congress determined to impose a cap and prevent climate catastrophe would have no choice but to nationalize the fossil-fuel industries, and the states would need to convert private gas, water, and electric (including renewable electric) utilities into locally controlled public utilities.

Imagine, if you will, that we do replace the fossil fuel giants with two brand-new public cooperatives—People's Carbon for coal and People's Hydrocarbon for oil and gas—whose mission is to put themselves out of business within the next decade or two. Their allocation of fuels would be conducted under democratic oversight nationally and administered locally. As the War Production Board did in the 1940s, the cooperatives will steer their diminishing allotments of fuels into society's various sectors, giving priority to renewable energy manufacturing and installation, providing sufficient supplies to critical direct uses such as home heating, steering fuels toward essential agriculture and manufacturing, and barring their use in wasteful or superfluous production. The production and allocation of concrete and steel will be similarly regulated. Dwindling supplies of fossil fuels will be allocated among local utilities to maintain adequate power generation, filling gaps not yet being filled by expanding non-fossil generation.

Meanwhile, contracts for the buildup of green infrastructure and wind and solar capacity will give preference to community and neighborhood power generation, prohibit profiteering, and contain provisions for limiting environmental harm. They will be steered away from large corporations as much as possible, and will strictly regulate inputs of materials and parts, barring suppliers who cause ecological or humanitarian damage anywhere in the country or world. The conversion to a new electric supply will occur more quickly in some regions than in others, but that doesn't matter as long as the national supply of fossil fuels is being both reduced on schedule and allocated where most needed.

At the same time, the Green New Deal's energy conservation provisions will kick off a national home-insulation and efficiency effort starting in lower-income neighborhoods, as well as an expansion of affordable housing and public transportation. There's a plan for this. In

November 2019, Congresswoman Ilhan Omar (D-Minn.) introduced an ambitious bill called the Homes for All Act, which would provide for 12 million affordable, environmentally sustainable housing units. The bill, she wrote, would be "a key part of the Green New Deal."[263]

With aviation fuel supplies dwindling, rail travel will replace air travel. High-speed, high-cost, high-concrete rail will be dropped from the transportation plan; instead, existing rail lines across the country will be refurbished and extended to carry modest-speed electric passenger and freight traffic, following a plan like the one urged today by the Solutionary Rail campaign.[264] Green public transportation within urban areas will be expanded, not by digging under the streets but by taking over existing streets and expressway lanes, gradually displacing private cars completely.

Both the IPCC and Green New Deal targets for driving down emissions would require a cap that reduces oil, gas, and coal use on a schedule so tight that new energy capacity can't be built and deployed fast enough to substitute fully for their retirement. Nationwide energy shortages will inevitably occur during the transition and beyond. No one wants to see a return of the panic and chaos that was triggered by the oil crisis and inflation of the 1970s. Well before any shortages arise, safety nets must be put in place. As use of oil, gas, and coal is phased out, the prices that both producers and consumers pay for fuel and electricity will rise, raising the risk of inflation throughout the economy. The government will likely have to impose price controls on all energy, as the Office of Price Administration did in the 1940s and the Nixon Administration did in the 1970s.

Price controls will keep the energy affordable, but they won't increase its supply. If there is not sufficient fuel or electricity to fully satisfy unchecked demand, a fair-shares rationing system will be needed in order to ensure that households have equitable access to electricity, gas, heating oil, and vehicle fuel. The simplest and fairest approach would be to allot to each household a monthly number of credits, free of charge, to be handed over when buying electricity and fuels. Those credits would be used like points in World War II–era meat rationing, when a household could buy only as much as its point coupons allowed. The numbers of credits issued to each person or household, to be handed over when paying utility bills or buying vehicle fuel or other energy products, would be determined each year according to the total quantities of electricity and fuels available under the national cap and allocated to the household sector.

Output from solar parks and wind farms will be increasing, but not as quickly as output from coal- and gas-fired power plants is decreasing under the cap. Therefore, it will be necessary to ration all electricity, whatever its source, to ensure fair shares of a limited supply. I suggest equal numbers of credits per adult for each energy source, with an additional half-credit each for up to two children per household.

In the industrial sector, national allocation of energy will help ward off shortages of essential goods, but as the fossil-fuel cap lowers, shortages of consumer goods could develop throughout the economy. At that point, a more comprehensive strategy to ensure fair shares and sufficiency for all will be needed. For several years, The Climate Mobilization has been working on just such a strategy as part of a "Victory Plan" through which the United States could effectively address the climate emergency and much more. The group has published drafts, most recently in 2019, but its plan continues to evolve.[265] Extraordinary in scope, it covers a phase-out of fossil fuels and a phase-in of alternative energy; a shift to public transportation; transformation of the food system; retrofitting of the built environment; redirection of the military toward an ecological mission; reforestation; research on reduction of atmospheric carbon; prevention of mass extinction; restoration of the oceans; and a socially just transition process.

The Victory Plan includes the general outlines of a cap-and-ration system for greenhouse emissions. (The plan's authors cite my book *Any Way You Slice It: The Past, Present and Future of Rationing* as a reference, but I was not involved in the plan's drafting.) Under the proposed mobilization, there would be a "rapidly declining national greenhouse gas emissions budget," that is, a declining cap. A point-based system would be used to rate all goods and services based on the emissions of greenhouse gases caused during their production and use. The rating system and cap would be applied in a stepwise fashion, first to the energy sector and somewhat later to transportation, manufacturing, and food. For each category of goods, an equal number of ration points would be issued to each household via a smart-card system. Households could sell unused rations back to the government for cash, and those rations would be retired.

Modeled in part on the civilian mobilization for World War II, the Victory Plan would be carried out by a broad array of agencies, including a Climate Mobilization Board, which would administer caps on fossil fuels and materials and oversee production goals. The Mobilization Board would be an analog of the War Production Board of the 1940s. Another agency from that era, the Office of Price Administration, would be revived under its original name to oversee price controls and rationing. Crucially, local residents would administer the rationing system in each community. A Mobilization Labor Board would ensure "true full employment," good wages, "paid family and medical leave, child care, healthcare benefits, and retirement benefits," and good-faith collective bargaining for the transition workforce.

A proposal focused more narrowly on fair-shares energy rationing is called Tradable Energy Quotas (TEQs). The system, which was developed over the past couple of decades by the U.K.-based Fleming Policy Center, was introduced, studied, and debated in Parliament in the 2000s, but it was judged to be ahead of its time. Now, with an emergency widely acknowledged, it warrants another look. I'm not saying that a Victory Plan or Tradable Energy Quotas should simply be copied and pasted into future policy; rather, I am using them as detailed examples of how fair-shares energy rationing can work at the household level.

Briefly, a Tradable Energy Quotas system would set up its version of a cap: a national carbon-emissions budget that declines year by year. Each fossil fuel would be assigned an emissions point value, and every household would have carbon accounts into which shares of carbon credits would be deposited weekly, with one share per household member. Each adult in the household would have an electronic, debit-type carbon card. Whenever drivers, for example, fill their cars' fuel tanks, they would pay the price of the fuel with cash or a credit card and also debit from the carbon card a number of TEQ credits corresponding to the number of carbon points carried by the fuel they just bought. Points for home electricity and natural gas could be automatically deducted from carbon accounts by the utilities just as they now deduct monthly bill payments from customers' bank accounts.[266]

As an emissions or fossil-energy cap ratchets downward and the substitution of renewable energy lags, people in specific situations—living far from work and unable to afford to live closer, perhaps, or living in a drafty house without having the money to insulate—may suffer a serious shortfall of ration credits. To address those situations, the proposal for tradable energy quotas would create a national market into which energy-efficient households can sell credits they don't need (for real money), and from which households can buy additional carbon credits if they run out before the next deposit arrives. The market is meant to help cover shortfalls, but by bringing cash back into the rationing system, a TEQ program might leave an opening for economic injustice to creep back into the system, increasing the cost of energy for low-income families while allowing affluent families to buy their way out of conservation. Larry Edwards has proposed an alternative process for filling the gaps. I won't get into the details here, but in his system, unused ration credits would automatically flow into a surplus pool from which people needing credits could draw for free, but in a way that responds to all requests uniformly up to an amount at which either the requests are all fulfilled or the credit pool is emptied.[267]

Whatever basic procedures and formulas end up being used for fair-shares energy rationing, they would need to be applied equitably throughout the nation. However, they could and should be administered locally, democratically, and inclusively, as is envisioned for Green New Deal policies. Local decision-making was a feature of both U.S. and U.K. rationing systems during World War II. More than five thousand local rationing boards, staffed by tens of thousands of paid employees and hundreds of thousands of volunteers, had, according to Amy Bentley in her book on wartime food rationing, "a significant amount of autonomy, enabling them to base decisions on local considerations."[268] While a cap on fossil fuels during the transition to renewable energy would affect everyone, how we use that energy should still be up to us, our neighbors, and our local communities. The national policy need not involve the government micromanaging our lives. We would know how much energy is available, and individuals and communities should be the ones who decide how to use their share. Police shouldn't be issuing tickets for "pleasure driving" as they did during World War II. Utilities shouldn't be remotely controlling our thermostat settings. No one should be telling us what we can or cannot eat. But we all will be living under the same energy limits.

When Green New Deal funds flow into communities for energy conservation and reduced dependence on fossil fuels, their use also should be determined by local, democratic, participatory processes. We should remember that when the New Deal faltered, the Southern Tenant Farmers Union, the West Coast dockworkers, and others stepped in to shake up the system and demand a course correction. Local and regional activism will almost certainly become important in seeing to it that national climate policy is applied fairly and effectively.

THE RISK IN "CLIMATE KEYNESIANISM"

House and Senate resolutions call for the Green New Deal to be developed through "transparent and inclusive consultation, collaboration, and partnership with frontline and vulnerable communities, labor unions, worker cooperatives, civil society groups, academia, and businesses." Funding would come largely from the federal government, but where would the government get the money? Such resolutions are not the place for specifics, so the documents have simply stated that Congress will provide capital for the Green New Deal in a way that "ensures that the public receives appropriate ownership stakes and returns on investment" through community grants, public banks, and other public financing. Congresswoman Alexandria Ocasio-Cortez, a sponsor of the House resolution, unleashed panic in the upper classes when she advocated that the United States raise additional revenue by bringing back the top income-tax rate of 70 percent or more that prevailed in the 1950s through the 1970s. Around the same time and unrelated to the Green New Deal, then-presidential contender Elizabeth Warren proposed a wealth tax that would apply to all personal assets in excess of $50 million.[269] More progressive taxes have been badly needed for decades, whatever the atmospheric CO_2 concentration, and the climate emergency could boost the movement for fairer taxation.

In May 2019, Yeva Nersisyan of Franklin & Marshall College and L. Randall Wray of Bard College published a paper, "How to Pay for the Green New Deal," its title echoing that of John Maynard Keynes's 1940 book *How to Pay for the War*. They argued that the U.S. government could handle the expense of the Green New Deal much more easily than it paid for the World War II effort, which from 1942 to 1945 consumed 35 to 45 percent of all federal spending. In fact, they showed how costs of the Green New Deal's big industrial effort and universal job guarantee, which would make up the bulk of the expense, could be largely paid for by cuts in military spending along with savings in administrative and drug costs under another big GND component, Medicare for All.[270]

Others have pointed to economic growth as a source of revenue. New Consensus, arguing that the Green New Deal could be paid for with "carefully targeted, Congressionally authorized spending," predicted that "the new prosperity that the Green New Deal will bring to scores of millions of Americans below the top of the income and wealth distributions will rapidly grow the nation's tax base, vastly expanding federal revenue even without raising marginal tax rates."[271] In 2019, a fact sheet accompanying the House resolution for the Green New Deal stated, "At the end of the day, this is an investment in our economy that should grow our wealth as a nation, so the question isn't how will we pay for it, but what will we do with our new shared prosperity."[272]

Paying for a green transition through economic growth sounds easy and painless, but it would be self-defeating. If, say, a twenty-five-year renewable buildup were to stimulate a consistent 3 percent growth rate in the broader economy, that would double the GDP within twenty-five years, swamping any achievements in decarbonization and energy efficiency.[273] As discussed in the previous chapter, renewable energy cannot support an economy's growth to that size and beyond. If we're expecting the just transition to increase prosperity, then we're going to need a new definition of prosperity. If emissions are going to be quickly brought under control, prosperity should not signify rising profits and growing wealth; rather, it should indicate the high degree of economic *and* ecological stability necessary to provide security for all, and excess for none. The Green New Deal was envisioned as a path to those goals, but aiming to "grow our wealth as a nation" will push demand for resources ever higher, making the renewable energy target harder to hit. That effort will fail in the end. Naomi Klein sums up the situation in her book *On Fire*:

> [A]ny credible Green New Deal needs a concrete plan for ensuring that the salaries from all the good green jobs it creates aren't immediately poured into high-consumer lifestyles that inadvertently end up increasing emissions—a scenario where everyone has a good job and lots of disposable income and it all gets spent on throwaway crap imported from China destined for the landfill. This is the problem with what we might call the emerging "climate Keynesianism": the post–World War II economic boom did revive ailing economies, but it also kicked off suburban sprawl and set off a consumption tidal wave that would eventually be exported to every corner of the globe. In truth, policymakers are still dancing around the question of whether we are talking about slapping solar panels on the roof of Walmart and calling it green, or whether we are ready to have a more probing conversation about the limits of lifestyles that treat shopping as the main way to form identity, community, and culture.[274]

In an ecologically rational economy, production must be reduced and redirected, not redoubled. The bulk of the employment, skills, facilities, and resources going into car, truck, and aircraft manufacturing can be redirected into solar and wind energy and public transportation. Construction currently dedicated to the wealth-oriented real estate industry can be redirected toward green infrastructure and retrofitting for energy efficiency, as well as affordable housing. And the Green New Deal's job guarantee could be fulfilled much more easily if the number of hours in a full-time workweek were reduced nationally.

THE 33 PERCENT

If we manage to achieve a fair, effective climate-emergency policy, the 33 percent of American households with highest incomes will most likely bear the greatest economic burden. I'm not just talking about more progressive tax rates; I'm suggesting that the kinds of efforts that will be most effective in reducing emissions while ensuring good quality of life for everyone will require a far greater economic sacrifice from the top 33 percent than from the rest of the population. And within that top one-third, the richer the household, the heavier the burden will have to be.

Thirty-three is not a magic number. But as we free ourselves from the catastrophic impact of fossil fuels, I would expect the actual percentage to end up within shouting distance of that figure. In his 2017 book *Dream Hoarders*, Richard Reeves suggests that the top 20 percent of income earners in the United States, those whom he calls the upper middle class, are unfairly garnering the lion's share of the nation's quality education, housing, health care, and other necessary goods and services. The remedies he suggested for this problem, he writes, will be costly, and the funding for them will have to come from those same top 20 percent.[275]

Future sacrifice should indeed come from the upper part of the economic pyramid, especially when a transition to social, racial, and economic justice are accepted as essential to a deep-green society. As we succeed in creating a more equitable, just, and ecologically sustainable society, the economy will come to look less like a pyramid and, as proposed by economist Kate Raworth, will better resemble a doughnut, with everyone living within its "safe and just space," neither in the "hole" of insufficiency nor in the ecologically insupportable space beyond the doughnut.[276]

For the sake of argument, let's say that taking this path will impact the top one-third of today's economic earners—those in households with incomes that annually exceed $95,000. Together, this one-third of U.S. households now receives two-thirds of the U.S. population's total income. The 33 percent owns 94 percent of stocks by value.[277] Their inflation-adjusted incomes are higher now than before the Great

Recession hit in 2008, while the other 67 percent's average income remains lower. The 33 percent have an average household net worth of approximately $700,000, in contrast to the 40 percent of households at the base of the economic pyramid whose average net worth is less than zero, at *negative* $22,000.[278] This country's 33 percenters are also 4 percenters, with higher incomes than 96 percent of the world's people. And 33 percent doesn't mean 33 for everyone. Only 18 percent of all Latinx households belong to the national top 33 percent for income, and only 15 percent of all Black households are members of that overall top third.[279]

The costs of the conversion to green energy capacity and infrastructure have been optimistically estimated at $15 trillion for the United States and $100 trillion globally[280]—and the latter will require a large U.S. contribution. No one really knows with any precision how much it will cost to stop global warming before it's too late, but I doubt that the eventual sum will be handled as casually as Nersisyan and Wray have predicted. The conversion required to free ourselves from fossil fuels will have to be heavily subsidized, with the money coming from taxation of higher incomes and deep cuts in military appropriations and other wasteful spending. And it will have to be regulated so that it provides plenty of employment and no profiteering.

To pay for the conversion, the more steeply progressive income tax rate suggested by Ocasio-Cortez will be necessary, but for the 33 percent, the bigger impacts will be indirect. Protecting the ecosphere from fossil fuels will initially impact most industries. Stock prices and corporate valuations will likely contract. Owners, investors, and upper managers, the great majority of whom belong to the 33 percent, will take a big hit. If the economy stagnates or if shortages and inflation strike, then price controls, subsidies, and other assistance will have to be directed at essential goods and vulnerable households. That will require even greater shifts of income and wealth from the 33 percent to the 67 percent.

For purposes of funding the transition, the largest contributor will be the ultra-rich one-percenters—1.2 million households—at the peak of the economic pyramid. This small group of Americans now earns approximately $1.8 trillion in annual income and pays $600 billion in taxes. Nevertheless, wealthy as they are, the one-percenters' contribution alone will not be sufficient to fund and sustain the conversion to a just and sustainable society. An additional 32 percent or more of high-earning households are going to have contribute as well.

This book is focused primarily on domestic climate policy, because neither we as individuals nor our government can, with a straight face, presume to advise the wider world on climate issues unless we ourselves have at least started the journey toward life within ecological boundaries. In preparing for that journey, we need to weigh the various actions that our country should pursue as it addresses the global climate emergency, as well as those it must abandon.

5

❧❦❧

JUSTICE FOR THE WHOLE EARTH

"One path, they said, would be well worn, but it would be scorched; the other path, they said, would not be well worn, it would be green."

—Winona LaDuke, citing Anishinaabe prophets, 2017[281]

It is important that the United States be engaged with the global South's climate emergency, most urgently by terminating the policies that have allowed our government and corporations to intervene in the South in many destructive ways. Furthermore, we have to push back against the old argument that even if we achieve good climate policy, all of the struggle and sacrifice will have gone for naught if the rest of the world continues to destabilize the Earth's biosphere. That's just an irrelevant excuse for doing nothing, and it needs to be confronted.

North America, Europe, Japan, and Australia together are responsible for 61 percent of all of the greenhouse contaminants that humanity has so far pumped into the atmosphere. Add India, China, and Russia, and the share rises to 85 percent.[282] Instead of being the deadbeat nation we are today, we could lead the way toward the ecological stabilization required for people—and all living things—to be more secure.

The economically poorest parts of the world—responsible for only 15 percent of global greenhouse emissions—are, tragically, where many of the worst impacts of climate change are being felt. If we succeed in managing U.S. greenhouse emissions properly, we will be doing more good for future generations in those countries than anything we've done for them so far. But it still won't cancel out the harm we've already done. John Bellamy Foster, Hannah Holleman, and Brett Clark observe that "plunder is a general phenomenon present to various degrees in relation to nearly all natural resources—whether gold, guano, oil, coffee, or soybeans—that are systematically drained from the global South by multinational corporations. The result is to impose enormous ecological and economic losses on poor, dependent countries."[283] We, the people of the United States, need to demand an end to that looting and to a lot more of what U.S. corporations and our government are doing. For starters, we can drive our national greenhouse emissions down to zero; stop treating the people of the global South as nothing more than cheap labor; shrink the U.S. military, then reorient what's left of it toward disaster prevention and relief;[284] and force financial institutions to forgive the debts of impoverished nations.

Once the United States has an airtight policy for driving down our own greenhouse emissions, we can enhance the system for imports to limit not only high-emissions goods but also much more of the wasteful and superfluous cargo we import. Patrick Moriarty warns, however, "Any growth slowdown will draw attention to distributional issues. 'Let them eat croissants' will no longer work. We have to be careful to ensure that adaptation and mitigation measures don't adversely affect the already badly-off, whether in the OECD [Organisation for Economic Co-operation and Development] or elsewhere."[285] To avoid harming working people in, say, China or Mexico as we cut our own consumption, we could strike new trade agreements that mandate living wages, international monitoring of mining sites (including in this country), and strict pollution controls on all factories, while favoring production that will help free societies from fossil-fuel use everywhere, rather than increasing energy demand. In a nod to increasing solar photovoltaic (PV) use, Congress could call it the "PVs, Not TVs Act of 2022."

THE GROUND TRUTH

Humanity will soon overshoot, or has already overshot, limits not only for greenhouse-gas accumulation but also for the Earth's nitrogen and phosphorus cycles, soil degradation, and biodiversity loss.[286] Human use of land has contributed heavily to all of those ecological crises and more. Settlement, industry, agriculture, livestock grazing, forestry, and other activities together now occupy more than 70 percent of the Earth's ice-free land surface, with big impacts not only on landscapes and waters but on greenhouse warming as well. In 2019, the Intergovernmental Panel on Climate Change followed up its blockbuster 1.5-degree report of the previous year with another focused on the impacts of land use on climate.[287] Almost one quarter of human-caused greenhouse-gas emissions, said the report, could be attributed to agriculture, forestry, and other land use. Those emissions, including carbon dioxide, methane, and nitrous oxide, have to be driven down as quickly as emissions from fossil fuels. Many of the same activities that are causing land-based emissions are taking a heavy toll on soil, water, ecosystems, and rural communities. Therefore, improvements in land use in both the North and the South can have positive effects that reach far beyond emissions reduction—if, that is, they are accomplished in non-exploitative ways.

The IPCC provided a long list of actions that together could slow global warming by reducing greenhouse-gas emissions while at the same time pulling carbon out of the atmosphere and storing it in plants and soil. Conservation of peatlands, wetlands, rangelands, mangroves, forests, and other ecosystems can store carbon. Restoring natural vegetation and reversing deforestation can and should be done across much larger areas of the Earth as well. However, notes the IPCC, reforestation, agroforestry, soil carbon management, and storing carbon in the form of wood products won't keep pulling carbon out of the atmosphere permanently. In contrast, they write, peatlands "can continue to sequester carbon for centuries." Reducing deforestation and forest degradation lowers greenhouse-gas emissions. Sustainable forest management can provide livelihoods and reduce the chance of deforestation. Food production can be made more ecologically sustainable by growing more perennial grains and pastures, reducing tillage, improving grazing and manure management, and controlling soil erosion. The bulk of the loss of soil carbon to the atmosphere has resulted from replacing perennial vegetation with annual crops and the repeated soil disturbance through tillage that annual crops require. The IPCC recommended reversing that process by replacing annual grain crops with perennial grains that are under development.[288]

Currently, says the IPCC, 25 to 30 percent of food produced worldwide is lost or wasted. Stopping that waste can reduce the land area devoted to cropping, thereby reducing emissions, and diversification in the food system will also have carbon benefits. They note, "Balanced diets, featuring plant-based foods, such as those based on coarse grains, legumes, fruits and vegetables, nuts and seeds, and animal-sourced food produced in resilient, sustainable and low-GHG emission systems, present major opportunities for adaptation and mitigation while generating significant co-benefits in terms of human health."

Reducing net emissions through land-use change involves practices that also restore ecosystem health, so almost all of its impacts on the landscape are positive. In other words, every land-use change that the IPCC says must be made for the sake of climate is something that we needed to be doing anyway for ourselves and the Earth as a whole.

There are many promising possibilities, but so far the global North has not played a constructive role in land-use change. Instead, we've been meddling in the South's land and energy management as part of the carbon-offsets shell games that are part of most mandatory cap-and-trade programs. Under an offset regime, a company such as an electric utility or airline can avoid buying permits by funding a project outside the system to reduce greenhouse emissions by, say, planting trees or decommissioning coal-fired power plants and substituting solar capacity. The most prominent offset program, the Clean Development Mechanism created by the Kyoto Protocol and long employed by Europe's carbon market, has been ineffective. An extensive independent study of the Mechanism found that 85 percent its offset projects did not deliver the advertised emissions reductions, or they sold credits for reductions that would have happened anyway without the Mechanism.[289] The state of California's cap-and-trade system also allows purchase of offsets, many of them spurious. One of its projects, which pays coal-mine owners to capture the methane they emit, would increase profits from coal mining by as much as 17 percent and could keep that dirty, economically stressed industry alive longer.[290]

Since 2007, the most prominent program for forest offsets has been the UN's Reducing Emissions from Deforestation and Forest Degradation (REDD). The program has come in for withering criticism over the years for its negative impacts on rural people of the global South and its failure to either preserve forests, address poverty, or provide climate benefits. *ProPublica* reporter Lisa Song investigated REDD offset projects around the world and reported in 2019 that she'd found they were, overall, a big washout. A long-term offset project launched in 2008, for example, was supposed to help Cambodian monks protect stretches of forests covering almost 250 square miles. The forests, however, were known to be vulnerable to military conflict and exploitation by loggers. *ProPublica* commissioned a satellite imagery analysis, finding that tree cover in the project area fell from 88 percent at the time of its launch to 46 percent in 2017.

Attempting to "decarbonize" the 2014 World Cup, the international soccer body FIFA bought credits from an offset project in the Brazilian state of Rondônia, home to the Paiter-Suruí tribe. The goal was to curb deforestation, but tribe members carefully documented the project's misspending of funds and failure to stop the logging. Funding was finally suspended in 2018 after the number of trees destroyed exceeded all of the credits that had been sold. Song cites a 2015 survey of 120 REDD projects by a French research organization, which showed that "REDD was simply layered onto existing conservation plans, reducing it to a 'logo to attract financing.'"[291]

From the tropics to the Arctic, it is Indigenous people who have been exploited and harmed the most by carbon offset projects, and it is Indigenous people who are pushing back hardest against them and their grim consequences. While attending the 2019 United Nations Conference of the Parties in Madrid (COP 25, the top annual international climate conference), a youth delegation representing the Canada-based network Indigenous Climate Action hand-delivered a letter to their minister of environment and climate, a climate negotiator. The letter expressed the concerns of Indigenous people in much of the world have about Article 6 of the Paris Agreement, the section that authorizes offsets and other transfers of emissions allowances among nations:

It is our view that in its current state, Article 6 does not promote viable climate solutions or the necessary human and Indigenous Rights protections to ensure true climate justice. Relying heavily on market-based solutions will only further delay the transition out of a fossil fuel economy while simultaneously allowing continued human and Indigenous rights abuses. There must be increased recognition of non-market solutions that are grounded in the Rights of Indigenous Peoples. It is well known that 80% of the world's biodiversity exists within recognized Indigenous lands and territories. In addition, the IPCC has also recognized carbon sinks are often located on Indigenous lands and territories. This is not happenstance, but is the result of millennia of stewardship founded in deep, spiritual connections with our lands and territories and not predicated on modern economic systems. We have proven our peoples' expertise and knowledge in developing successful non-market solutions that surpass current carbon market mechanisms. For these reasons, our rights are essential to mitigating emissions, protecting critical biodiversity and upholding tenets of climate justice.[292]

As the youth delegates pointed out, the very concept of offsets is not only unjust but also incompatible with the sure, rapid elimination of fossil fuels. Forests in Brazil absolutely must be protected, and community solar projects should proliferate in Pakistan. Such efforts merit support, but that support should never be used as an excuse for burning fossil fuels elsewhere. Kevin Anderson, a leading climate scholar and activist, deplores offsets. He has written, "Offsetting is worse than doing nothing. It is without scientific legitimacy, is dangerously misleading, and almost certainly contributes to a net increase in the absolute rate of global emissions growth."[293]

BETWEEN THE FLOOR AND THE CEILING

The thorniest issue in international climate negotiations has been the question of how to divide up the decreasing number of tons of emissions that can be released worldwide each year and still remain on schedule to hold global warming to an acceptable limit. The world's nations could commit, for example, to allocate permitted emissions in proportion to the current output of each nation—a simple but extremely unfair formula that has been called the "grandfathering rule." Another simple, fairer, but imperfect plan would be to allocate emissions rights on a per-capita basis. Alternatively, a universal per-capita emissions ceiling could be established annually, and all nations would have to get themselves under the ceiling while also establishing a floor, that is, ensuring a minimum energy supply sufficient to provide good quality of life for everyone.[294] There are other types of criteria, as well as many possibilities for devising hybrids of two or more criteria.

Philosophers and ethicists have argued, based on principles of distributive justice, that what should be allocated fairly is not emissions but lifetime *benefits derived from emissions*, with equal shares for every Earthling now alive. In our lifetimes, people in affluent countries, on average, have benefited more from their own greenhouse emissions than have others, and they have benefited more from past emissions generated by industrialization. Therefore, to level out the benefits, historically high-emitting countries should be allowed a smaller per capita share of the declining future-emissions budget, while less developed countries should be allowed a larger share.[295]

This question of carving up the emissions pie among nations is complex enough. But how to reduce the huge disparities that exist within nations regarding both the benefits and the harm that people have derived from capitalism, growth, and greenhouse emissions, both present and past? And how to prevail over the elites in every country, large or small, North or South, who will resist any change in the status quo that would redistribute power or resources to the majority?

The Ireland-based climate group Feasta has a plan called Cap Global Carbon that would operate similarly to James Boyce's cap-and-permit strategy discussed in Chapter 3, but on a worldwide scale. A number of permits for the global carbon budget would be auctioned off to fossil-fuel companies, and sale of any quantity of fuel without corresponding permits would be prohibited worldwide. Companies would pass the permit costs down the line to customers, while a Global Climate Commons Trust would administer the system and rebate revenues from the auction globally in equal per-person shares.[296] Cap Global Carbon suffers from the same uncertainties and inequities that affect any system that puts a price on carbon, and its rebate system would only obliquely address the huge disparities in economic power and energy access that exist among and within nations. Its argument for global fair-shares energy allocation is a good first step, but as in our own domestic policy, fairer and more direct mechanisms for fossil-fuel suppression are needed.

Climate actions such as those I have proposed for the United States couldn't simply be transplanted elsewhere, but some economic justice elements, modified to be locally appropriate, could be useful. The Green New Deal aims to raise the economic floor for all Americans through its pro-worker, pro-poor economic provisions, while steeply progressive income and wealth taxes would help lower both the economic and emissions ceilings. Some form of cap-and-ration policy that redirects energy and other resources toward what people need and away from opulence would further raise the floor and lower the ceiling.

In the highly integrated global economy, the downsizing of wealth among America's 33 percent can help downsize wealth among upper economic tiers in developing countries as well. For example, if the United States can free itself from fossil fuels and strategically downsize production, the example may inspire big countries such as China and India, as well as smaller nations. Getting private cars off the road and aircraft out of the sky while expanding public transportation and establishing a ceiling and floor for household energy consumption would bother only the elites and benefit the great majority of people in the South. Low-income countries could also shift the climate mitigation burden to the upper classes, who consume the most resources. Meanwhile, climate mitigation through better land use as urged by the IPCC—for example, through soil-conserving production of diverse food crops and sustainable forest and grassland management—would benefit not only the atmosphere but all those who live and work on the land.

BEYOND DENIAL, WHETHER HARD OR SOFT

We in the United States have frittered away more than three decades in avoiding action on climate, for fear of slowing down "the economy"—shorthand for slowing down resource extraction and capital accumulation. Within a neoliberal vision, the range of acceptable actions addressing any environmental or social problem is limited to those that benefit "the economy." To be acceptable, an action has to be positive or at least neutral with regard to economic growth, not only eventually, but most importantly in the coming fiscal year or quarter. We have arrived at the point where continuing to ignore the intensifying climate emergency for the sake of short-term economic growth will itself melt down "the economy" in the medium or long term. It will also sink any chance that the world's increasingly vulnerable majority—those who keep "the economy" going, with very little to show for it—might have at a safer, better life.

Since 1992, the guardians of economic growth and George Bush Sr.'s "American way of life" have fed on the denial of human-induced climate change that remains endemic among conservatives. Now, however, at a time when we have finally achieved fairly broad agreement that the fact of greenhouse warming cannot plausibly be dismissed, the climate movement is facing what could be an even bigger challenge than traditional climate denial. Writing for *New Economic Perspectives* in 2016, Michael Hoexter characterized our current condition as one of "soft climate denial," which, he wrote, "is defined by the disconnect between the recognition of an apparent climate emergency and the psychological repression or the dismissal of appropriate responses to that emergency."[297] It is to pretend, writes British Green Party politician Rupert Read, "that we can keep making cake together, even though the ingredients are running out and the kitchen is filling up with smoke."[298] Most political decision-makers who would never have denied the reality of human-induced climate change are nevertheless in soft climate denial, incrementally accepting that greenhouse warming is a threat to human life and health—and even to civilization itself—but pretending that economically acceptable half-measures will take care of the problem.

We now have the best opportunity yet to break through both hard and soft denial and get something real done. Greenhouse warming has been steadily climbing the list of politically urgent priorities since about 2016, especially since the IPCC's October 2018 report. The Green New Deal and climate-emergency movements have ridden the wave of activism to good effect, preparing public consciousness to demand bold climate legislation no matter which political bias dominates Congress, the White House, and the courts. Ambitious, effective climate action is growing more politically popular every day. It is up to each and everyone of us to insist that our public servants in Washington enact ecologically necessary legislation on a crash timetable. The time to free ourselves from fossil fuels is now.

To squander this opportunity would be to stay the course on the road to ruin. We all must block out pro-corporate cost-benefit analyses, nuclear enthusiasts' peril-plagued prescriptions, ecomodernists' siren songs, and Silicon Valley's relentless technocentric boosterism. Above all, we must refute the soft climate deniers' blithe reassurances that economic growth without limit can coexist with an effective struggle to end greenhouse warming. Expansion of the human economy is going to end, one way or the other. No one can predict when or where the road to ecological reality will begin or whether it will be voluntary or imposed upon us by circumstances. How growth ends—democratically, fairly, and peacefully, or in a manner more like a remake of the dystopian classic *Mad Max* shot in a sauna—will be largely determined not in that still fairly distant time but now, and through next decade, maybe two. Winona LaDuke vividly describes the decision that lies before us:

> In our teachings as an Anishinaabe people, where we are now is referred to as the time of the Seventh Fire. It is said that long ago prophets came to our people—the same prophets who instructed us specifically where to go—and they said that at the Time of the Seventh Fire, we as Anishinaabe people would have a choice between two paths. One path, they said, would be well worn, but it would be scorched; the other path, they said, would not be well worn, it would be green. It would be

our choice upon which path to embark. Frankly, I'm pretty sure that's where we all are now. We're at a moment in time when we have the ability to stop the prevailing white-men mentality from combusting the planet to oblivion. . . . We have a shot at stopping some pretty extreme behavior at the end of the cannibal or Wiindigoo economy. This, in my estimation, is a great spiritual opportunity for us all."[299]

We could ignore ecological necessity and drive on past the exit ramp. No one can predict exactly how that would end, but I don't think we want to run the experiment and find out. If on the other hand we do take the exit, can we get oil, gas, and coal out of our life fast enough? There are several credible definitions of "fast enough," but it doesn't matter which we aim for. The necessity will be the same: to free ourselves from fossil fuels as soon as we can, to establish ecological stability, and to ensure fair shares for all. We don't know exactly how that will turn out either. But maybe if we do it, the Earth that our generations leave behind, though gravely wounded, will remain livable.

ACKNOWLEDGMENTS

I am deeply grateful to Joseph Nevins, who set in motion the events that led to this book and provided valuable feedback on the manuscript; to Greg Ruggiero of City Lights, whose editing prowess made this book what it is; and to all of the folks who have helped me learn and think about these issues and/or provided advice on the manuscript: Wes Jackson, Robert Jensen, Justin Podur, Sheila Cox, Paul Cox, Larry Edwards, Shaun Chamberlain, Lisi Krall, Riccardo Mastini, Don Fitz, Ezra Silk, Margaret Salamon, and Laura Berry. Finally, I want to thank Priti Gulati Cox, the love of my life, without whom this book would not exist.

APPENDIX 1

COMPLETE TEXT OF HOUSE RESOLUTION 109
Introduced in the House January 3, 2019

116TH CONGRESS
1ST SESSION H. RES. 109

*Recognizing the duty of the Federal Government
to create a Green New Deal.*

IN THE HOUSE OF REPRESENTATIVES

Ms. OCASIO-CORTEZ submitted the following resolution;
which was referred to the Committee

RESOLUTION

Recognizing the duty of the Federal Government
to create a Green New Deal.

Whereas the October 2018 report entitled "Special Report on Global Warming of 1.5° C" by the intergovernmental Panel on Climate Change and the November 2018 Fourth National Climate Assessment report found that—

• human activity is the dominant cause of observed climate change over the past century;

- a changing climate is causing sea levels to rise and an increase in wild-fires, severe storms, droughts, and other extreme weather events that threaten human life, healthy communities, and critical infrastructure
- global warming at or above 2 degrees Celsius beyond preindustrial-ized levels will cause—
  - mass migration from the regions most affected by climate change;
  - more than $500,000,000,000 in lost annual economic output in the United States by the year 2100;
  - wildfires that, by 2050, will annually burn at least twice as much forest area in the western United States than was typically burned by wildfires in the years preceding 2019;
  - a loss of more than 99 percent of all coral reefs on Earth;
  - more than 350,000,000 more people to be exposed globally to deadly heat stress by 2050; and
  - a risk of damage to $1,000,000,000,000 of public infrastructure and coastal real estate in the
  - United States; and
  - global temperatures must be kept below 1.5 degrees Celsius above preindustrialized levels to avoid the most severe impacts of a changing climate, which will require—
  - global reductions in greenhouse gas emissions from human sources of 40 to 60 percent from 2010 levels by 2030; and net-zero emis-sions by 2050;

Whereas, because the United States has historically been responsible for a disproportionate amount of greenhouse gas emissions, having emitted 20 percent of global greenhouse gas emissions through 2014, and has a high technological capacity, the United States must take a leading role in reducing emissions through economic transformation;

Whereas the United States is currently experiencing several related crises, with—

- life expectancy declining while basic needs, such as clean air, clean water, healthy food, and adequate health care, housing, transporta-tion, and education, are inaccessible to a significant portion of the United States population;

- a 4-decade trend of economic stagnation, deindustrialization, and antilabor policies that has led to—
- hourly wages overall stagnating since the 1970s despite increased worker productivity;
  - the third-worst level of socioeconomic mobility in the developed world before the Great Recession
  - the erosion of the earning and bargaining power of workers in the United States; and
  - inadequate resources for public sector workers to confront the challenges of climate change at local, State, and Federal levels; and
  - the greatest income inequality since the 1920s, with—
  - the top 1 percent of earners accruing 91 percent of gains in the first few years of economic recovery after the Great Recession;
  - a large racial wealth divide amounting to a difference of 20 times more wealth between the average White family and the average Black family; and
  - a gender earnings gap that results in women earning approximately 80 percent as much as men, at the median;

Whereas climate change, pollution, and environmental destruction have exacerbated systemic racial, regional, social, environmental, and economic injustices (referred to in this preamble as "systemic injustices") by disproportionately affecting indigenous communities, communities of color, migrant communities, deindustrialized communities, depopulated rural communities, the poor, low-income workers, women, the elderly, the unhoused, people with disabilities, and youth (referred to in this preamble as "frontline and vulnerable communities");

Whereas, climate change constitutes a direct threat to the national security of the United States—

- by impacting the economic, environmental, and social stability of countries and communities around the world; and
- by acting as a threat multiplier;

Whereas the Federal Government-led mobilizations during World War II and the New Deal created the greatest middle class that the United

States has ever seen, but many members of frontline and vulnerable communities were excluded from many of the economic and societal benefits of those mobilizations; and

Whereas the House of Representatives recognizes that a new national, social, industrial, and economic mobilization on a scale not seen since World War II and the New Deal is a historic opportunity—

- to create millions of good, high-wage jobs in the United States;
- to provide unprecedented levels of prosperity and economic security for all people of the United States; and
- to counteract systemic injustices:

Now, therefore, be it

Resolved, That it is the sense of the House of Representatives that—

- it is the duty of the Federal Government to create a Green New Deal—
  - to achieve net-zero greenhouse gas emissions through a fair and just transition for all communities and workers;
  - to create millions of good, high-wage jobs and ensure prosperity and economic security for all people of the United States;
  - to invest in the infrastructure and industry of the United States to sustainably meet the challenges of the 21st century;
  - to secure for all people of the United States for generations to come—
    (i)   clean air and water;
    (ii) climate and community resiliency;
    (iii) healthy food;
    (iv) access to nature; and
    (v)   a sustainable environment; and
  - to promote justice and equity by stopping current, preventing future, and repairing historic oppression of indigenous communities, communities of color, migrant communities, deindustrialized communities, depopulated rural communities, the poor, low-income workers, women, the elderly, the unhoused, people with

disabilities, and youth (referred to in this resolution as "frontline and vulnerable communities");

- the goals described in subparagraphs of paragraph (1) above (referred to in this

- resolution as the "Green New Deal goals") should be accomplished through a 10-year national mobilization (referred to in this resolution as the "Green New Deal mobilization") that will require the following goals and projects—

  – building resiliency against climate change-related disasters, such as extreme weather, including by leveraging funding and providing investments for community-defined projects and strategies;

  – repairing and upgrading the infrastructure in the United States, including—

    (i) by eliminating pollution and greenhouse gas emissions as much as technologically feasible;

    (ii) by guaranteeing universal access to clean water;

    (iii) by reducing the risks posed by flooding and other climate impacts; and

    (iv) by ensuring that any infrastructure bill considered by Congress addresses climate change;

  – meeting 100 percent of the power demand in the United States through clean, renewable, and zero-emission energy sources, including—

    (i) by dramatically expanding and upgrading existing renewable power sources; and

    (ii) by deploying new capacity;

  – building or upgrading to energy-efficient, distributed, and "smart" power grids, and working to ensure affordable access to electricity;

  – upgrading all existing buildings in the United States and building new buildings to achieve maximal energy efficiency, water efficiency, safety, affordability, comfort, and durability, including through electrification;

  – spurring massive growth in clean manufacturing in the United States and removing pollution and greenhouse gas emissions from manufacturing and industry as much as is technologically feasible, including by expanding renewable energy manufacturing and investing in existing manufacturing and industry;

— working collaboratively with farmers and ranchers in the United States to eliminate pollution and greenhouse gas emissions from the agricultural sector as much as is technologically feasible, including—

(i)   by supporting family farming;

(ii) by investing in sustainable farming and land use practices that increase soil health; and

(iii) by building a more sustainable food system that ensures universal access to healthy food;

— overhauling transportation systems in the United States to eliminate pollution and greenhouse gas emissions from the transportation sector as much as is technologically feasible, including through investment in—

(i)   zero-emission vehicle infrastructure and manufacturing;

(ii) clean, affordable, and accessible public transportation; and

(iii) high-speed rail;

— mitigating and managing the long-term adverse health, economic, and other effects of pollution and climate change, including by providing funding for community-defined projects and strategies;

— removing greenhouse gases from the atmosphere and reducing pollution, including by restoring natural ecosystems through proven low-tech solutions that increase soil carbon storage, such as preservation and afforestation;

— restoring and protecting threatened, endangered, and fragile ecosystems through locally appropriate and science-based projects that enhance biodiversity and support climate resiliency;

— cleaning up existing hazardous waste and abandoned sites to promote economic development and sustainability;

— identifying other emission and pollution sources and creating solutions to eliminate them; and

- promoting the international exchange of technology, expertise, products, funding, and services, with the aim of making the United States the international leader on climate action, and to help other countries achieve a Green New Deal;

• a Green New Deal must be developed through transparent and inclusive consultation, collaboration, and partnership with frontline and vulnerable communities, labor unions, worker cooperatives, civil society groups, academia, and businesses; and

• to achieve the Green New Deal goals and mobilization, a Green New Deal will require the following goals and projects—

- providing and leveraging, in a way that ensures that the public receives appropriate ownership stakes and returns on investment, adequate capital (including through community grants, public banks, and other public financing), technical expertise, supporting policies, and other forms of assistance to communities, organizations, Federal, State, and local government agencies, and businesses working on the Green New Deal mobilization;

- ensuring that the Federal Government takes into account the complete environmental and social costs and impacts of emissions through—

  (i) existing laws;

  (ii) new policies and programs; and

  (iii) ensuring that frontline and vulnerable communities shall not be adversely affected;

- providing resources, training, and high-quality education, including higher education, to all people of the United States, with a focus on frontline and vulnerable communities, so those communities may be full and equal participants in the Green New Deal mobilization;

- making public investments in the research and development of new clean and renewable energy technologies and industries;

- directing investments to spur economic development, deepen and diversify industry in local and regional economies, and build wealth and community ownership, while prioritizing high-quality

job creation and economic, social, and environmental benefits in
frontline and vulnerable communities that may otherwise struggle
with the transition away from greenhouse gas intensive industries;

– ensuring the use of democratic and participatory processes that
are inclusive of and led by frontline and vulnerable communities
and workers to plan, implement, and administer the Green New
Deal mobilization at the local level;

– ensuring that the Green New Deal mobilization creates high-
quality union jobs that pay prevailing wages, hires local workers,
offers training and advancement opportunities, and guarantees
wage and benefit parity for workers affected by the transition;

– guaranteeing a job with a family-sustaining wage, adequate family
and medical leave, paid vacations, and retirement security to all
people of the United States;

– strengthening and protecting the right of all workers to organize,
unionize, and collectively bargain free of coercion, intimidation,
and harassment;

– strengthening and enforcing labor, workplace health and safety,
antidiscrimination, and wage and hour standards across all employers, industries, and sectors;

– enacting and enforcing trade rules, procurement standards,
and border adjustments with strong labor and environmental
protections—

  (i) to stop the transfer of jobs and pollution overseas; and

  (ii) to grow domestic manufacturing in the United States;

– ensuring that public lands, waters, and oceans are protected and
that eminent domain is not abused;

– obtaining the free, prior, and informed consent of indigenous
people for all decisions that affect indigenous people and their
traditional territories, honoring all treaties and agreements with
indigenous people, and protecting and enforcing the sovereignty
and land rights of indigenous people;

– ensuring a commercial environment where every businessperson is free from unfair competition and domination by domestic or international monopolies; and

– providing all people of the United States with—

   (i)   high-quality health care;

   (ii) affordable, safe, and adequate housing;

   (iii) economic security; and

   (iv) access to clean water, clean air, healthy and affordable food, and nature.

APPENDIX 2

COMPLETE TEXT OF HOUSE RESOLUTION 52

Introduced in the House July 9, 2019

116TH Congress 1ST SESSION H. CON. RES. 52

Expressing the sense of Congress that there is a climate emergency which demands a massive-scale mobilization to halt, reverse, and address its consequences and causes.

IN THE HOUSE OF REPRESENTATIVES
July 9, 2019

Mr. Blumenauer (for himself, Ms. Ocasio-Cortez, Ms. Lee of California, Ms. Jayapal, Ms. Norton, Mr. Espaillat, Mrs. Watson Coleman, Ms. Velázquez, Ms. Haaland, Mr. Neguse, Mr. Smith of Washington, Mr. Grijalva, Ms. Pressley, Ms. Omar, Mrs. Napolitano, Mr. Heck, Mr. DeFazio, Mr. Brendan F. Boyle of Pennsylvania, Mr. Levin of Michigan, Ms. Schakowsky, Mr. Ted Lieu of California, Mr. Cohen, Mr. Nadler, Mr. Raskin, Mr. Serrano, Mr. Larson of Connecticut, Ms. Clarke of New York, Mr. Higgins of New York, Ms. Barragán, Ms. Meng, Mr. Sherman, Mr. McGovern, Mrs. Lowey, and Mr. Suozzi) submitted the following concurrent resolution; which was referred to the Committee on Energy and Commerce

CONCURRENT RESOLUTION

Expressing the sense of Congress that there is a climate emergency which demands a massive-scale mobilization to halt, reverse, and address its consequences and causes.

Whereas 2015, 2016, 2017, and 2018 were the 4 hottest years on record and the 20 warmest years on record have occurred within the past 22 years;

Whereas global atmospheric concentrations of the primary heat-trapping gas, or greenhouse gas, carbon dioxide—

(1) have increased by 40 percent since preindustrial times, from 280 parts per million to 415 parts per million, primarily due to human activities, including burning fossil fuels and deforestation;

(2) are rising at a rate of 2 to 3 parts per million annually; and

(3) must be reduced to not more than 350 parts per million, and likely lower, "if humanity wishes to preserve a planet similar to that on which civilization developed and to which life on Earth is adapted," according to former National Aeronautics and Space Administration climatologist, Dr. James Hansen;

Whereas global atmospheric concentrations of other greenhouse gases, including methane, nitrous oxide, and hydrofluorocarbons, have also increased substantially since preindustrial times, primarily due to human activities, including burning fossil fuels;

Whereas current climate science and real-world observations of climate change impacts, including ocean warming, ocean acidification, floods, droughts, wildfires, and extreme weather, demonstrate that a global rise in temperatures of 1 degree Celsius above preindustrial levels is already having dangerous impacts on human populations and the environment;

Whereas the 2018 National Climate Assessment found that climate change due to global warming has caused, and is expected to cause additional, substantial interference with and growing losses to infrastructure, property, industry, recreation, natural resources, agricultural systems, human health and safety, and quality of life in the United States;

Whereas the National Oceanic and Atmospheric Administration has determined that climate change is already increasing the frequency of extreme weather and other climate-related disasters, including drought, wildfire, and storms that include precipitation;

Whereas climate-related natural disasters have increased exponentially over the past decade, costing the United States more than double the long-term average during the period of 2014 through 2018, with total costs of natural disasters during that period of approximately $100,000,000,000 per year;

Whereas the Centers for Disease Control and Prevention has found wide-ranging, acute, and fatal public health consequences from climate change that impact communities across the United States;

Whereas the National Climate and Health Assessment of the United States Global Change Research Program identified climate change as a significant threat to the health of the people of the United States, leading to increased—

(1) temperature-related deaths and illnesses;

(2) air quality impacts;

(3) extreme weather events;

(4) numbers of vector-borne diseases;

(5) waterborne illnesses;

(6) food safety, nutrition, and distribution complications; and

(7) mental health and well-being concerns;

Whereas the consequences of climate change already disproportionately impact frontline communities and endanger populations made especially vulnerable by existing exposure to extreme weather events, such as children, the elderly, and individuals with pre-existing disabilities and health conditions;

Whereas individuals and families on the frontlines of climate change across the United States, including territories, living with income inequality and poverty, institutional racism, inequity on the basis of gender and sexual orientation, poor infrastructure, and lack of access to health care, housing, clean water, and food security are often in close proximity to environmental stressors or sources of pollution, particularly communities of color, indigenous communities, and low-income communities, which—

(1) experience outsized risk because of the close proximity of the community to environmental hazards and stressors, in addition to collocation with waste and other sources of pollution;

(2) are often the first exposed to the impacts of climate change; and

(3) have the fewest resources to mitigate those impacts or to relocate, which will exacerbate preexisting challenges;

Whereas, according to Dr. Robert Bullard and Dr. Beverly Wright, "environmental and public health threats from natural and human-made disasters are not randomly distributed," therefore a response to the climate emergency necessitates the adoption of just community transition policies and processes available to all communities, which include policies and processes rooted in principles of racial equity, self-determination, and democracy, as well as the fundamental human right of all people to clean air and water, healthy food, adequate land, education, and shelter;

Whereas climate change holds grave and immediate consequences not just for the population of the United States, including territories, but for communities across the world, particularly those communities in the Global South on the frontlines of the climate crisis that are at risk of forced displacement;

Whereas communities in rural, urban, and suburban areas are all dramatically affected by climate change, though the specific economic, health, social, and environmental impacts may be different;

Whereas the Department of State, the Department of Defense, and the intelligence community have identified climate change as a threat to national security, and the Department of Homeland Security views climate change as a top homeland security risk;

Whereas climate change is a threat multiplier—

(1) with the potential to exacerbate many of the challenges the United States already confronts, including conflicts over scarce resources, conditions conducive to violent extremism, and the spread of infectious diseases; and

(2) because climate change has the potential to produce new, unforeseeable challenges in the future;

Whereas, in 2018, the United Nations Intergovernmental Panel on Climate Change projected that the Earth could warm 1.5 degrees Celsius above preindustrial levels as early as 2030;

Whereas the climatic changes resulting from global warming above 1.5 degrees Celsius above preindustrial levels, including changes resulting from global warming of more than 2 degrees Celsius above preindustrial levels, are projected to result in irreversible, catastrophic changes to public health, livelihoods, quality of life, food security, water supplies, human security, and economic growth;

Whereas, in 2019, the United Nations Intergovernmental Science-Policy Platform on Biodiversity and Ecosystem Services found that human-induced climate change is pushing the planet toward the sixth mass species extinction, which threatens the food security, water supply, and well-being of billions of people;

Whereas, according to climate scientists, limiting global warming to not more than 1.5 degrees Celsius above preindustrial levels, and likely lower, is most likely to avoid irreversible and catastrophic climate change;

Whereas, even with global warming up to 1.5 degrees Celsius above preindustrial levels, the planet is projected to experience—

(1) a significant rise in sea levels;

(2) extraordinary loss of biodiversity; and

(3) intensifying droughts, prodigious floods, devastating wildfires, and other extreme weather events;

Whereas, according to climate scientists, addressing the climate emergency will require an economically just and managed phase-out of the use of oil, gas, and coal to keep fossil fuels in the ground;

· Whereas the United Nations Intergovernmental Panel on Climate Change has determined that limiting warming through emissions reduction and carbon sequestration will require rapid, and immediate, acceleration and proliferation of "far-reaching, multilevel, and cross-sectoral climate mitigation" and "transitions in energy, land, urban and rural infrastructure (including transport and buildings), and industrial systems";

Whereas, in the United States, massive, comprehensive, and urgent governmental action is required immediately to achieve the transitions of those systems in response to the severe existing and projected economic, social, public health, and national security threats posed by the climate crisis;

Whereas the massive scope and scale of action necessary to stabilize the climate will require unprecedented levels of public awareness, engagement, and deliberation to develop and implement effective, just, and equitable policies to address the climate crisis;

Whereas failure to mobilize and solve the climate emergency is antithetical to the spirit of the Declaration of Independence in protecting "unalienable Rights" that include "Life, Liberty and the pursuit of Happiness";

Whereas the United States has a proud history of collaborative, constructive, massive-scale Federal mobilizations of resources and labor in order to solve great challenges, such as the Interstate Highway System, the Apollo 11 Moon landing, Reconstruction, the New Deal, and World War II;

Whereas the United States stands uniquely poised to substantially grow the economy and attain social and health benefits from a massive mobilization of resources and labor that far outweigh the costs of inaction;

Whereas millions of middle class jobs can be created by raising labor standards through project labor agreements and protecting and expanding the right of workers to organize so that workers in the United States and the communities of those workers are guaranteed a strong, viable economic future in a zero-emissions economy that guarantees good jobs at fair union wages, with quality benefits;

Whereas frontline communities, Tribal governments and communities, people of color, and labor unions must be equitably and actively engaged in the climate mobilization and prioritized through local climate mitigation and adaptation planning, policy, and program delivery so that workers in the United States, [and] the communities of those workers, are guaranteed a strong, viable economic future;

Whereas a number of local jurisdictions and governments in the United States, including New York City and Los Angeles, and across the world, including the United Kingdom, the Republic of Ireland, Portugal, and Canada, have already declared a climate emergency, and a number of State and local governments are considering declaring a climate emergency in response to the massive challenges posed by the climate crisis;

Whereas State, local, and Tribal governments must be supported in efforts to hold to account actors whose activities have deepened and accelerated the climate crisis and who have benefitted from delayed action to address the climate change emergency and to develop a fossil fuel-free economy;

Whereas a collaborative response to the climate crisis will require the Federal Government to work with international, State, and local governments, including with those governments that have declared a climate emergency, to reverse the impacts of the climate crisis; and

Whereas the United States has an obligation, as a driver of accelerated climate change, to mobilize at emergency speed to restore a safe climate and environment not just for communities of the United States, including territories, but for communities across the world, particularly those on the frontlines of the climate crisis who have least contributed to the crisis, and to account for global and community impacts of any actions it takes in response to the climate crisis: Now, therefore, be it

Resolved by the House of Representatives (the Senate concurring), That it is the sense of Congress that—

(1) the global warming caused by human activities, which increase emissions of greenhouse gases, has resulted in a climate emergency that—

(A) severely and urgently impacts the economic and social well-being, health and safety, and national security of the United States; and

(B) demands a national, social, industrial, and economic mobilization of the resources and labor of the United States at a massive scale to halt, reverse, mitigate, and prepare for the consequences of the climate emergency and to restore the climate for future generations; and

(2) nothing in this concurrent resolution constitutes a declaration of a national emergency for purposes of any Act of Congress authorizing the exercise, during the period of a national emergency or other type of declared emergency, of any special or extraordinary power.

ENDNOTES

1. Henry Fountain, "Climate Change Is Accelerating, Bringing World 'Dangerously Close' to Irreversible Change," *New York Times*, December 5, 2019, A10.

2. Oded Carmelie, "'The Sea Will Get as Hot as a Jacuzzi': What Life in Israel Will Be Like in 2100," *Haaretz*, August 17, 2019, www.haaretz.com/israel-news/.premium.MAGAZINE-the-sea-will-get-as-hot-as-a-jacuzzi-what-life-in-israel-will-look-like-in-2100-1.7688062.

3. The IPCC was created in 1988 by the World Meteorological Organization and the United Nations Environment Program. It draws on the work of thousands of scientists worldwide to supply governments with up-to-date scientific evaluations and projections regarding the global climate. Its website is ipcc.ch.

4. IPCC, *Global Warming of 1.5° C*, October 2018, www.ipcc.ch/sr15.

5. United Nations Environment Programme, "Emissions Gap Report 2019," November 26, 2019, unenvironment.org/resources/emissions-gap-report-2019.

6. See Chapter 3 for more on energy transitions. Also see Richard York and Shannon Elizabeth Bell, "Energy Transitions or Additions? Why a Transition from Fossil Fuels Requires More Than the Growth of Renewable Energy," *Energy Research and Social Science* 51 (2019): 40–43.

7. Giorgos Kallis, "A Green New Deal Must Not Be Tied to Economic Growth," *Truthout*, March 10, 2019.

8. As in previous reports, the IPCC relied only on published studies and analyses regarded as scientifically solid and was cautious in its conclusions. While potentially on the conservative side, the report's still-jarring projections make the broadest and most authoritative case for policies and direct mechanisms that will clamp down on emissions as hard and as rapidly as possible.

9. IPCC, *Global Warming of 1.5° C*. Even with 1.5° of warming, twice as many megacities will experience severe heat stress, exposing more than 350 million more people to deadly heat by 2050. At 2°, Pakistan and India could see an annual reoccurrence of the unprecedented heat waves that killed more than four thousand people in 2015.

10. IPCC finds that each degree Celsius increase in global mean temperature is projected to reduce production of wheat by 6 percent, rice by 3 percent, maize by 7.4 percent, and soybeans by 3 percent, on average. In the greater Mekong region of Southeast Asia, rice yield losses per degree of warming could exceed 10 percent. The report predicts that total human impact of drought will grow by 64 percent. Southeast Asia's crop production could drop by one-third. A large increase in loss of fisheries can be expected.

11. Naomi Klein, "A Message From the Future with Alexandria Ocasio-Cortez," *The Intercept*, April 17, 2019.

12. Mark Lynas, *Six Degrees: Our Future on a Hotter Planet* (Washington, DC: National Geographic, 2008); David Wallace-Wells, *The Uninhabitable Earth: Life After Warming* (New York: Tim Duggan, 2019).

13. Donella Meadows, Dennis Meadows, Jørgen Randers, and William Behrens III, *The Limits to Growth* (New York: Universe, 1972).

14. Arthur Ekirch Jr., *Ideologies and Utopias: The Impact of the New Deal on American Thought* (Chicago: Quadrangle, 1969), 83–84.

15. Renshaw, "Was There a Keynesian Economy in the USA Between 1933 and 1945?" *Journal of Contemporary History* 34 (1999): 337–64.

16. Ira Katznelson, *Fear Itself: The New Deal and the Origins of Our Time* (New York: Liveright, 2013), 229–235, 244.

17. Ibid., 244.

18. Don Worster, *Dust Bowl: The Southern Plains in the 1930s* (New York: Oxford University Press, 1979), 11, 15, 38.

19. Worster, *Dust Bowl*, 44.

20. McLeman, Robert A., Juliette Dupre, Lea Berrang Ford, James Ford, Konrad Gajewski, and Gregory Marchildon, "What We Learned from the Dust Bowl: Lessons in Science, Policy, and Adaptation," *Population and Environment* 35 (2014): 417–40.

21. Natural Resources Conservation Service, "History of NRCS," www.nrcs.usda.gov/wps/portal/nrcs/main/national/about/history/. The Soil Conservation Service was renamed as the Natural Resources Conservation Service in 1994.

22. Neil Maher, "'Crazy Quilt Farming on Round Land:' The Great Depression, the Soil Conservation Service, and the Politics of Landscape Change on the Great Plains During the New Deal Era," *Western Historical Quarterly* 31 (2000): 319–39.

23. Neil Maher, "A New Deal Body Politic: Landscape, Labor, and the Civilian Conservation Corps," *Environmental History* 7 (2002): 435–61.

24. Theda Skocpol and Kenneth Finegold, "State Capacity and Economic Intervention in the Early New Deal," *Political Science Quarterly* 97 (1982): 255–78.

25. Michael Goldfield, "Worker Insurgency, Radical Organization, and New Deal Labor Legislation," *American Political Science Review* 83 (1989): 1257–82.

26. Ibid.

27. Federal Housing Administration, Underwriting Manual, Underwriting and Valuation Procedure Under Title II of the National Housing Act, Washington, D.C., US. Government Printing Office, 1938, www.huduser.gov/portal/sites/default/files/pdf/Federal-Housing-Administration-Underwriting-Manual.pdf.

28. Steve Valocchi, "The Racial Basis of Capitalism and the State, and the Impact of the New Deal on African Americans," *Social Problems* 41 (1994): 347–62.

29. Jerold Auerbach, "Southern Tenant Farmers: Socialist Critics of the New Deal," *Arkansas Historical Quarterly* 27 (1968): 113–31. Auerbach reports that although the STFU was a thoroughly interracial organization, it still existed in the 1930s South; therefore, each local tended to have either all Black or all white membership.

30. Ibid.

31. Ibid.

32. Ibid.

33. Ibid.

34. See James Whitman, "Of Corporatism, Fascism and the First New Deal" (1991), *Faculty Scholarship Series*, No. 660, digitalcommons.law.yale.edu/fss_papers/660; and John Garraty, "The New Deal, National Socialism, and the Great Depression," *American Historical Review* (1973): 907–44.

35. Peter Beinert, "Is Donald Trump a Fascist?" *New York Times*, September 11, 2018.

36. Renshaw, "Was There a Keynesian Economy?" He adds, "Many accept that it was American involvement in the Second World War, not New Deal policies, which ended the mass unemployment of the 1930s. Fewer understand that it was spending on war in 1914–18 and 1941–45 (and one might add in Vietnam in the 1960s), not spending on social or welfare reform at any time, which created the public debt conservatives criticized so angrily in the 1980s."

37. Ibid.

38. Hugh Rockoff, *Drastic Measures: A History of Wage and Price Controls in the United States* (Cambridge: Cambridge University Press, 1984), 85–126.

39. Ibid.

40. Ibid.

41. Ibid.

42. Rockoff, *Drastic Measures*, 130; *Victory Bulletin*, April 3, 1944.

43. Amy Bentley, *Eating for Victory: Food Rationing and the Politics of Domesticity* (Champaign: University of Illinois Press, 1998), 22–24.

44. See, e.g., Table E1 in U.S. Energy Information Administration, "Annual Energy Review," September, 2012, www.eia.gov/totalenergy/data/annual/showtext.php?t=ptb1601.

45. Paul Baran and Paul Sweezy, *Monopoly Capital: An Essay on the Economic and Social Order* (New York: Monthly Review Press, 1966).

46. For a summary of *Monopoly Capital* on its fifty-year anniversary and its impact on economics and society, see John Bellamy Foster, "*Monopoly Capital* at the Half-Century Mark," *Monthly Review* 68 (2016): 1–25.

47. "Transcript of Nixon's Acceptance Address and Excerpts From Agnew's Speech," *New York Times*, August 24, 1972.

48. "Business Briefs," *New York Times*, September 21, 1972.

49. Meadows et al., *Limits to Growth.*

50. Graham Turner, "A Comparison of *The Limits to Growth* with 30 Years of Reality," *Global Environmental Change* 18 (2008): 397–411; Charles Hall and John Day, "Revisiting *The Limits to Growth* After Peak Oil," *American Scientist* 97 (2009): 230–37.

51. In considering any attempt to overcome natural limits with technology, the *Limits to Growth* authors asked, "Is it better to try to live within that limit by accepting a self-imposed restriction on growth? Is it preferable to go on growing until some other natural limit arises, in the hope that at that time another technological leap will allow growth to continue still longer? For the last several hundred years human society has followed the second course so consistently and successfully that the first choice has been all but forgotten." Ibid., 141, 152–53.

52. Turner, "A Comparison;" Hall and Day, "Revisiting."

53. Associated Press, "Some Questions and Answers on Heating Oil Rationing Plan," *Argus-Press* (Owasso, MI), November 28, 1973.

54. Shane Hamilton, "The Populist Appeal of Deregulation: Independent Truckers and the Politics of Free Enterprise, 1935–1980," *Enterprise & Society* 10 (2009): 137–77.

55. Jefferson Cowie, *Stayin' Alive: The 1970s and the Last Days of the Working Class* (New York: The New Press, 2010), 224–25.

56. Daniel Horowitz, *Jimmy Carter and the Energy Crisis of the 1970s: The "Crisis of Confidence" Speech of July 15, 1979; A Brief History with Documents* (Boston: St. Martins, 2005), 111.

57. Hamilton, "Populist Appeal."

58. Jimmy Carter, speech, July 15, 1979, www.c-span.org/video/?153917-1/president-carter-address-crisis-confidence.

59. Kevin Mattson, *What the Heck Are You Up To, Mr. President? Jimmy Carter, America's "Malaise," and the Speech That Should Have Changed the Country* (New York: Bloomsbury, 2009), 156–159.

60. Ross Cheit, "The Energy Mobilization Board," *Ecology Law Quarterly* 8 (1980): 727–47.

61. Horowitz, *Jimmy Carter.*

62. Images of U.S. Gasoline Rationing Coupons are posted on the website of the Smithsonian National Postal Museum: postalmuseum.si.edu/collections/object-spotlight/gas-coupons.html.

63. U.S. Department of Energy, *Standby Gasoline Rationing Plan* (Springfield, VA: NTIS, 1980), ntl.bts.gov/lib/12000/12200/12291/12291.pdf.

64. United Press International, "Rationing Coupons Shredded," *New York Times*, June 2, 1984.

65. Cowie, *Stayin' Alive*, 225.

66. For the calculation method, as applied to the years 1980–2012, see Stan Cox, *Any Way You Slice It: The Past, Present, and Future of Rationing* (New York: The New Press, 2013), 272, note 107.

67. James Everett Katz, "U.S. Energy Policy Impact of the Reagan Administration," *Energy Policy* 12 (1984): 135–45.

68. *Securing America's Energy Future: National Energy Policy Plan* (Washington, DC: U.S. Dept. of Energy, 1981).

69. Katz, "U.S. Energy Policy."

70. Ibid.

71. James Hansen et al., "Target Atmospheric CO_2: Where Should Humanity Aim?" *Open Atmospheric Science Journal* 2 (2008): 217–31.

72. "A Greener Bush," *The Economist*, February 13, 2003.

73. See tables at Bureau of Economic Analysis, "GDP and Personal Income," apps.bea.gov/iTable/index_nipa.cfm, undated.

74. Helen Dewar and Kevin Sullivan, "Senate Republicans Call Kyoto Pact Dead," *Washington Post*, December 11, 1997.

75. Richard Stevenson and Alan Cowell, "Bush Arrives at Summit Session, Ready to Stand Alone," *New York Times*, July 7, 2005.

76. Geoffrey Lean, "A 'Green New Deal' Can Save the World's Economy, Says UN," *The Independent*, October 12, 2008.

77. "At Climate Talks, a Few Letters That Almost Sank the Deal," *New York Times*, December 14, 2015.

78. "Statement by President Trump on the Paris Climate Accord," The White House, June 1, 2017, whitehouse.gov/briefings-statements/statement -president-trump-paris-climate-accord.

79. Margaret Salamon, interview by the author, April 5, 2019.

80. Ezra Silk, interview by the author, April 5, 2019.

81. Ezra Silk, "The Climate Mobilization Victory Plan," theclimatemobil ization.org/victory-plan.

82. Umair Irfan, "'Climate Change' and 'Global Warming' Are Disappearing from Government Websites," *Vox*, November 9, 2017, www.vox .com/energy-and-environment/2017/11/9/16619120/trump-administration -removing-climate-change-epa-online-website.

83. Justin Worland, "Wildfires, Flooding and Droughts Could Make Climate Change an Issue in 2020. Some Are Pushing for It to Be the Top One," *Time*, March 5, 2019.

84. White House, "Remarks by the President on the Paris Agreement," October 5, 2016, obamawhitehouse.archives.gov/the-press-office/2016/10/05/ remarks-president-paris-agreement.

85. C-SPAN, "Russell Greene Gets Climate Mobilization Into Democratic Platform," July 9, 2016, c-span.org/video/?c4779211/russell-greene-climate-mobilization-democratic-platform.

86. Kelly Hayes, "Standing Rock and the Power and Determination of Indigenous America," *Pacific Standard*, September 7, 2018.

87. Arnold Shroder, "On Direct Action with Trump Around," *Portland Rising Tide*, December 1, 2016, portlandrisingtide.org/direct-action-trump-around.

88. *America's Pledge: Phase 1 Report* (New York: Bloomberg Philanthropies, 2017), 127.

89. "The Climate Mobilization Begins in Los Angeles!," The Climate Mobilization blog, October 15, 2017, theclimatemobilization.org/blog/2018/4/25/the-climate-mobilization-begins-in-los-angeles.

90. "S-987–100 by '50 Act," 115th Congress, April 27, 2017, www.congress.gov/bill/115th-congress/senate-bill/987.

91. Jeff Merkley, "The Most Ambitious Piece of Climate Legislation Congress Has Ever Seen," *350.org*, April 15, 2017, 350.org/the-most-ambitious-climate-legislation-congress-has-seen/.

92. Eugene Robinson, "Yes, the Green New Deal Is Audacious. But We Have No Choice but to Think Big," *Washington Post*, February 18, 2019.

93. H. Damon Matthews, "Quantifying Historical Carbon and Climate Debts among Nations," *Nature Climate Change* 6 (2015): 60.

94. Jenny Staletovich, "Maria Death Toll Likely Topped 4,000 in Puerto Rico, 70 Times Official Count, Study Finds," *Miami Herald*, May 29, 2018.

95. Gloria Guzman, "U.S. Median Household Income Up in 2018 From 2017," U.S. Census Bureau, September 26, 2019, census.gov/library/stories/2019/09/us-median-household-income-up-in-2018-from-2017.html; "Puerto Rico," The Central Intelligence Agency World Factbook, November 20, 2019, cia.gov/library/publications/resources/the-world-factbook/geos/rq.html.

96. Jeff Stein, Tracy Jan, and Josh Dawsey, "HUD Inspector General's Office Says It'll Look into Whether White House Interfered with Puerto Rico Disaster Aid," *Washington Post*, March 26, 2019.

97. David Dayen, "Trump Administration Tells Puerto Rico It's Too Rich for Aid Money," *The Intercept*, January 18, 2018; Jeff Stein and Josh Dawsey, "Puerto Rico Faces Food-Stamp Crisis as Trump Privately Vents about Federal Aid to Hurricane Maria-Battered Island," *Washington Post*, March 25, 2019.

98. Natasha Lycia Ora Bannan, "Puerto Rico's Odious Debt: The Economic Crisis Of Colonialism," *CUNY Law Review* 19 (2018): 287–311.

99. "New Census Data on Puerto Rico," *Puerto Rico Report*, December 19, 2016, puertoricoreport.com/new-census-data-puerto-rico; "U.S. Census Bureau QuickFacts: Puerto Rico," undated, census.gov/quickfacts/PR.

100. For a firsthand look at Sierra Brava a year and a half after Maria, see Stan Cox and Paul Cox, "In Salinas, Puerto Rico, Vulnerable Americans Are Still Trapped in the Ruins Left by Hurricane Maria," *CounterPunch*, March 15,

2019. For related images, see Priti Gulati Cox, "Living Here and Not in the Street Is Worth Gold," *Sidewalk Museum of Congress*, March 10, 2019, pritigcox .wordpress.com/2019/03/10/living-here-and-not-in-the-street-is-worth-gold/.

101. Naomi Klein, *The Battle for Paradise: Puerto Rico Takes on the Disaster Capitalists* (Chicago: Haymarket, 2018).

102. James Ellsmoor, "Puerto Rico Has Just Passed Its Own Green New Deal," *Forbes*, March 25, 2019.

103. When a magnitude-6.4 earthquake hit the island's southwest coast in early 2020, the Trump administration approved a measly $5 million in emergency funds. Meanwhile, it continued to sit on 3,600 times that amount of aid: $18 billion that had been appropriated by Congress after Maria but remained locked away in Washington; Erica Werner, "Hit by Devastating Earthquakes, Puerto Rico Still Waiting on Billions for Hurricane Relief," *Washington Post*, January 9, 2020.

104. Barack Obama, "The Irreversible Momentum of Clean Energy," *Science* 355(2009): 126–129.

105. Daniel Cooper, "A Renewable Planet Is Almost Inevitable," *Engadget*, March 18, 2017, engadget.com/2017/03/08/a-renewable-planet-is -almost-inevitable/.

106. Dominic Dudley, "Renewable Energy Will Be Consistently Cheaper Than Fossil Fuels by 2020, Report Claims," *Forbes*, January 13, 2018.

107. William J. Barber II, "We are Witnessing the Birth Pangs of a Third Reconstruction," *Think Progress*, December 15, 2016.

108. Kyle Moore, "375 Arrested for Week Five of the Poor People's Campaign," *Medium*, June 13, 2018.

109. Saurav Sarkar and Shailly Gupta Barnes, "The Souls of Poor Folks," Institute for Policy Studies, April, 2018, ips-dc.org/souls-of-poor-folks.

110. Intergovernmental Panel on Climate Change, *Global Warming of 1.5° C*, October, 2018, www.ipcc.ch/sr15.

111. Ezra Silk, interview by the author, April 5, 2019.

112. Thomas Friedman, "The Green New Deal Rises Again," *New York Times*, January 8, 2019.

113. Colin Hines, "Seeing Off the Brexit Blues with a Green New Deal," *Brave New Europe*, March 29, 2019, braveneweurope.com/colin-hines-seeing -off-the-brexit-blues-with-a-green-new-deal.

114. Pettifor would later publish a book on the subject: Ann Pettifor, *The Case for the Green New Deal* (New York: Verso, 2019). In it, she focused on economics, advocating for public control of the financial system and a steady-state economy. See Bart Hawkins Kreps, "Platforms for a Green New Deal," *An Outside Chance*, October 31, 2019, anoutsidechance.com/2019/10/31/ platforms-for-a-green-new-deal/.

115. Hines, "Seeing."

116. Greg Carlock and Emily Mangan, "A Green New Deal," Data for Progress, September, 2018, dataforprogress.org/green-new-deal.

117. New Consensus, "The Green New Deal: Mobilizing for a Just, Prosperous, and Sustainable Economy," January 2019, newconsensus.com/wp-content/uploads/2019/02/new_consensus_gnd_14_pager.pdf.

118. Ellie Shechet, "The 'Extinction Rebellion' Wants You to Wake Up," *Rolling Stone*, January 28, 2019.

119. Extinction Rebellion, rebellion.earth/.

120. Brahmjot Kaur, "Over 60 Climate Change Activists Arrested In NYC 'Die-In'," *Gothamist*, April 17, 2019.

121. Miranda Green, "Ocasio-Cortez Joins Climate Change Sit-in at Pelosi's Office," *The Hill*, November 13, 2018.

122. Margaret Salamon, interview by the author, April 5, 2019.

123. Damian Carrington, "School Climate Strikes: 1.4 Million People Took Part, Say Campaigners," *The Guardian*, March 19, 2019.

124. Youth Climate Strike, youthclimatestrikeus.org/platform.

125. Sarah Kaplan, "How a 7th-Grader's Strike against Climate Change Exploded into a Movement," *Washington Post*, February 15, 2019.

126. Robinson Meyer, "A Centuries-Old Idea Could Revolutionize Climate Policy," *The Atlantic*, February 19, 2019.

127. Michael Grunwald, "The Trouble With the 'Green New Deal,'" *Politico*, January 25, 2019.

128. Kate Aronoff, Alyssa Battistoni, Daniel Aldana Cohen, and Thea Riofrancos, "A Green New Deal to Win Back Our Future," *Jacobin*, February 5, 2019.

129. Adam Rogers, "The Green New Deal Shows How Grand Climate Politics Can Be," *Wired*, February 8, 2019.

130. "Bill McKibben: Green New Deal Is a Chance to 'Remake Not Just a Broken Planet, But a Broken Society,' *Democracy Now!*, April 15, 2019.

131. Dino Grandoni, "Trump Keeps Inventing New Details About the Green New Deal," *Washington Post*, April 8, 2019.

132. The Climate Mobilization, "Green New Deal Is a Breakthrough," February 7, 2019, theclimatemobilization.org/blog/green-new-deal-is-a-break through.

133. Giorgos Kallis, "A Green New Deal Must Not Be Tied to Economic Growth," *Truthout*, March 10, 2019.

134. Vaios Triantafyllou, "A Green New Deal Is the First Step Toward an Eco-Revolution," *Truthout*, February 9, 2019.

135. Kate Aronoff, "How to Bury the Fossil Fuel Industry," *In These Times*, April 22, 2019.

136. Greenpeace USA, "Green New Deal Still Needs to Face Fossil Fuel Industry," press release, February 7, 2019, greenpeace.org/usa/news/breaking-green-new-deal-still-needs-to-face-fossil-fuel-industry/.

137. "Talking Points on the AOC-Markey Green New Deal (GND) Resolution," Indigenous Environmental Network, undated, www.ienearth.org/green-new-deal/.

138. Jason Hickel, "Climate Breakdown Is Coming. The UK Needs a Greener New Deal," *The Guardian*, March 5, 2019.

139. William Barber and Liz Theoharis, "By Striking for the Climate, We're Striking Against Poverty and Racism Too," *Newsweek*, September 20, 2019.

140. Bill McKibben, "A World at War," *Rolling Stone*, August 15, 2016.

141. Mark Jacobson Mark Delucchi, Zack Bauer, et al., "100% Clean and Renewable Wind, Water, and Sunlight All-Sector Energy Roadmaps for 139 Countries of the World," *Joule* 1 (2017): 108–21.

142. As I have noted, I usually avoid the term renewable energy, but "100 percent renewable" is the only convenient general term for the scenarios of Jacobson et al. and others that refer to themselves as proposals for 100 percent renewable energy.

143. Benjamin Heard, Barry Brook, Tom Wigley, and Corey Bradshaw, "Burden of Proof: A Comprehensive Review of the Feasibility of 100% Renewable-Electricity Systems," *Renewable and Sustainable Energy Reviews* 76 (2017): 1122–33. The authors used their analysis to support continued use of nuclear energy, which should be opposed for many reasons. But that does not undercut their critique of the 100 percent renewable scenarios.

144. Christopher Clack, Staffan Qvist, Jay Apt, et al., "Evaluation of a Proposal for Reliable Low-Cost Grid Power with 100% Wind, Water, and Solar," *Proceedings of the National Academy of Sciences* 114 (2017): 6722–27, critiquing Mark Jacobson, Mark Delucchi, Mary Cameron, and Bethany Frew, "Low-Cost Solution to the Grid Reliability Problem with 100% Penetration of Intermittent Wind, Water, and Solar for All Purposes," *Proceedings of the National Academy of Sciences* 112 (2015): 15060–65.

145. Peter Loftus, Armond Cohen, Jane Long, and Jesse Jenkins, "A Critical Review of Global Decarbonization Scenarios: What Do They Tell Us About Feasibility?" *Climate Change* 6 (2015): 93–112.

146. Mark Jacobson, Mark Delucchi, Mary Cameron, and Brian Mathiesen, "Matching Demand with Supply at Low Cost in 139 Countries Among 20 World Regions with 100% Intermittent Wind, Water, and Sunlight (WWS) for All Purposes," *Renewable Energy* 123 (2018): 236–48. Because of the damage they do to rivers, ecosystems, and human communities, hydroelectric dams and reservoirs should never be classified as "green" or "renewable" energy sources. See, for example, D. M. Rosenberg, R. A. Bodaly, and Peter Usher, "Environmental and Social Impacts of Large Scale Hydroelectric Development: Who Is Listening?" *Global Environmental Change* 5 (1995): 127–48.

147. Jan Christoph Steckel, Robert Brecha, Michael Jakob, Jessica Strefler, and Gunnar Luderer, "Development Without Energy? Assessing Future Scenarios of Energy Consumption in Developing Countries," *Ecological*

Economics 90 (2013): 53–67. The watt is a measure of the energy flux through a system, defined as one joule per second.

148. John Morrow, Jr. and Julie Ann Smith-Morrow, "Switzerland and the 2,000-Watt Society," *Sustainability* 1 (2008): 32–33.

149. Jacobson et al., "Matching"; wattages in this table are from Table S5 in the paper's supplementary materials.

150. Steckel et al., "Development Without Energy?"

151. One of the best statistical expositions of the need for evening out global energy/emissions disparities is Shoibal Chakravarty, Ananth Chikkatur, Heleen De Coninck, Stephen Pacala, Robert Socolow, and Massimo Tavoni, "Sharing Global CO_2 Emission Reductions Among One Billion High Emitters," *Proceedings of the National Academy of Sciences* 106 (2009): 11884–88.

152. Clack et al., "Evaluation."

153. Jacobson's fifteen-fold increase in the rate of buildup, unrealistic as it is, seems to be a solid estimate of what's needed. To substitute renewable electricity for fossil-fired electricity, as well as all burning of fossil fuels for heat, transportation, manufacturing, etc. by 2050 would require a buildup of solar-plus-wind energy output at eleven times America's highest rate of increase in output, which occurred in the years 2015–18; doing it by 2030 would require a thirty-three-fold increase in the rate. On top of that would be the daunting task of building a new national power distribution system and adapting heating, transportation, manufacturing, and agriculture to run entirely on electricity. Compensating fully for a fossil-fuel drawdown worldwide would require renewable capacity to be increasing by 7.3 to 11.6 trillion watts annually in the 2030s—in other words, every year *seven to eleven times* as much renewable capacity as exists worldwide today would have to be installed; Sgouris Sgouridis, Denes Csala, and Ugo Bardi, "The Sower's Way: Quantifying the Narrowing Net-Energy Pathways to a Global Energy Transition," *Environmental Research Letters* 11 (2016): 094009; "World Reaches 1,000GW of Wind and Solar, Keeps Going," *Bloomberg New Energy Finance*, August 2, 2018, https://about .bnef.com/blog/world-reaches-1000gw-wind-solar-keeps-going.

154. As renewable energy capacity expands, its net energy output per acre of land will decline. That's because once the windiest or sunniest locations have been exploited, further capacity will have to be installed on successively less windy or sunny landscapes that will yield fewer and fewer watts per square meter; however, the amount of energy required to construct the parks and farms will not decrease. Net energy capacity will continue to grow, but more slowly than the growth of the wind and solar industries would suggest. At some point, no further growth of net energy will be possible. See Patrick Moriarty and Damon Honnery. "Can Renewable Energy Power the Future?" *Energy Policy* 93 (2016): 3–7.

155. Carlos De Castro, Margarita Mediavilla, Luis Javier Miguel, and Fernando Frechoso, "Global Solar Electric Potential: A Review of Their

Technical and Sustainable Limits," *Renewable and Sustainable Energy Reviews* 28 (2013): 824–35.

156. Carlos De Castro, Margarita Mediavilla, Luis Javier Miguel, and Fernando Frechoso, "Global Wind Power Potential: Physical and Technological Limits," *Energy Policy* 39 (2011): 6677–82.

157. Clack, "Evaluation."

158. Patrick Moriarty and Damon Honnery, "Ecosystem Maintenance Energy and the Need for a Green EROI," *Energy Policy* 131 (2019): 229–34.

159. The IPCC urged this in its landmark 2019 report: IPCC, "Climate Change and Land," August 7, 2019, www.ipcc.ch/report/srccl/; see Chapter Five.

160. Moriarty and Honnery, "Global Potential."

161. John Asafu-Adjaye et al., "An Ecomodernist Manifesto," April 2015, ecomodernism.org.

162. Aaron Bastani, *Fully Automated Luxury Communism: A Manifesto* (New York: Verso, 2019); Aaron Bastani, "The World Is a Mess. We Need Fully Automated Luxury Communism," *New York Times*, June 11, 2019; Brian Merchant, "Fully Automated Luxury Communism," *The Guardian*, March 18, 2015.

163. See the short version here: Jeremy Caradonna et al., "A Degrowth Response to an Ecomodernist Manifesto," *Resilience*, May 6, 2015; the full document is here: resilience.org/articles/General/2015/05_May/A-Degrowth-Response-to-An-Ecomodernist-Manifesto.pdf.

164. In rejecting nuclear energy, the rebuttal cited the tiny share of the world's energy that nuclear had provided compared with the damage it had caused; the excessive cost in money and greenhouse emissions of any attempt to build up large nuclear capacity; its dependence on mining of uranium; its inextricable links with nuclear weapons; the inaccessibility of nuclear in much of the world; the impossibility of safely storing nuclear wastes for the necessary ten thousand years; and the inevitability of further catastrophic accidents at nuclear power plants and sites where radioactive nuclear wastes are stored.

165. Aaron Vansintjan, "Where's the 'Eco' in Ecomodernism?" *Red Pepper*, April 4, 2018, redpepper.org.uk/wheres-the-eco-in-ecomodernism/.

166. David Roberts, "Scientists Assessed the Options for Growing Nuclear Power. They Are Grim," *Vox*, July 11, 2018.

167. M. Granger Morgan, Ahmed Abdulla, Michael Ford, and Michael Rath, "US Nuclear Power: The Vanishing Low-Carbon Wedge," *Proceedings of the National Academy of Sciences* 115 (2018): 7184–89.

168. Regarding these and other issues, see John Bellamy Foster's takedown of ecomodernism: John Bellamy Foster, "The Long Ecological Revolution," *Monthly Review*, November 2017.

169. Backing up a system like that on a continental scale, however, would have to achieve eye-popping levels of storage capacity. One desktop simulation

of a U.S.-wide effort to supply 72 GW reliably using only wind and solar would require a system capable of producing 200 GW, along with the capacity to store a staggering 875 GWh of electricity supply. Even then, there still would be outages. Cory Budischak, DeAnna Sewell, Heather Thomson, Leon Mach, Dana Veron, and Willett Kempton, "Cost-Minimized Combinations of Wind Power, Solar Power and Electrochemical Storage, Powering the Grid Up to 99.9% of the Time," *Journal of Power Sources* 225 (2013): 60–74.

170. William Pickard, "Smart Grids Versus the Achilles' Heel of Renewable Energy: Can the Needed Storage Infrastructure Be Constructed Before the Fossil Fuel Runs Out?" *Proceedings of the IEEE* 102 (2014): 1094–1105.

171. Mathilde Fajardy and Niall Mac Dowell, "The Energy Return on Investment of BECCS: Is BECCS a Threat to Energy Security?," *Energy & Environmental Science* 11 (2018): 1581–94.

172. Alice Larkin, Jaise Kuriakose, Maria Sharmina, and Kevin Anderson, "What if negative emission technologies fail at scale? Implications of the Paris Agreement for big emitting nations," *Climate Policy* 18 (2018): 690–714.

173. It requires more energy to capture and store a ton of CO_2 from the air than a coal plant generates in the process of emitting a ton into the air. Conceptually, therefore, as many coal plants would be needed to pull CO_2 out of the atmosphere as were responsible for putting it into the atmosphere. And then their own emissions would have to be captured before going out the smokestack. For emissions from natural gas–fired generation, which has lower carbon intensity, "only" half as many capturing plants as emitting plants would be needed. Daniel Krekel, Remzi Can Samsun, Ralf Peters, and Detlef Stolten, "The Separation of CO_2 from Ambient Air—A Techno-Economic Assessment," *Applied Energy* 218 (2018): 61–381; Moriarty and Honnery, "Ecosystem Maintenance." The latter authors note that "although a renewable-energy plant could be used to run the capture plant, there would be no point in using renewable energy for the direct-air capture plants, since it would be far cheaper to use the renewable energy directly, thus saving DAC plant expenditure and CO_2 'burial.'" Moriarty told me, "Everybody talks about direct-air capture, but nobody is going to do it, because of the energy requirements." Patrick Moriarty, phone interview with author, June 24, 2019.

174. Felix Creutzig, "Economic and Ecological Views on Climate Change Mitigation with Bioenergy and Negative Emissions," *GCB Bioenergy* 8 (2016): 4–10; Wil Burns and Simon Nicholson, "Bioenergy and Carbon Capture with Storage (BECCS): The Prospects and Challenges of an Emerging Climate Policy Response," *Journal of Environmental Studies and Sciences* 7 (2017): 527–34; Paul Williamson, "Scrutinize CO_2 Removal Methods," *Nature* 530 (2016): 153-55; Pete Smith, Stephen Davis, Felix Creutzig, et al., "Biophysical and Economic Limits to Negative CO_2 Emissions," *Nature Climate Change*, 6 (2016): 42–60. To make matters worse, most models that include bioenergy assume that crop breeders and agronomists will achieve unrealistically rapid increases in

productivity of both food crops and energy crops; therefore, they underestimate the amount of additional land that will have to be brought under cultivation. Smith et al. conclude that attempts to maximize yields of bioenergy crops on vast acreages could double the world's use of nitrogen fertilizer. Use of synthetic fertilizers in agriculture worldwide has already doubled the quantity of reactive nitrogen compounds that naturally occur in the Earth's air, lands, and waters, with devastating ecological consequences, including greenhouse warming. At the same time, hundreds of millions of farmers in low-income countries are obtaining low crop yields because they can't afford enough fertilizer.

175. Loftus et al., "Critical Review."

176. In 2017, Elon Musk, the founder of the high-end electric car company Tesla, was being criticized for starting the company for the purpose of taking advantage of government subsidies. On Twitter, he denied the charge, writing that he had been inspired by the award-winning 2006 documentary *Who Killed the Electric Car?*, which followed General Motors' ill-fated marketing of its electric EV1 model in California. Lauren Thomas, "Elon Musk: We Started Tesla after Big Auto Companies Tried to 'Kill' the Electric Car," *CNBC*, June 9, 2017, www.cnbc.com/2017/06/09/elon-musk-i-started-tesla-after-detroit-tried-to-kill-electric-cars.html.

177. Troy Hawkins, Bhawna Singh, Guillaume Majeau-Bettez, and Anders Hammer Strømman, "Comparative Environmental Life Cycle Assessment of Conventional and Electric Vehicles," *Journal of Industrial Ecology* 17 (2013): 53–64. The study finds that, all factors considered, the lifetime emissions of an electric vehicle drawing on an electric grid that's still powered predominantly by natural gas and coal is similar to the lifetime emissions of a gas or diesel vehicle.

178. Ibid.

179. Charles Lane, "Why Electric Cars Still Don't Live up to the Hype," *Washington Post*, December 30, 2019.

180. We can partially compensate for the additional electricity used for heating by doing away with unnecessary over-air-conditioning; Stan Cox, *Losing Our Cool: Uncomfortable Truths About Our Air-Conditioned World* (New York: The New Press, 2010), 36–43.

181. Grandell, Leena, Antti Lehtilä, Mari Kivinen, Tiina Koljonen, Susanna Kihlman, and Laura Lauri, "Role of Critical Metals in the Future Markets of Clean Energy Technologies," *Renewable Energy* 95 (2016): 53–62.

182. Damien Giurco, Elsa Dominish, Nick Florin, Takuma Watari, and Benjamin McLellan, "Requirements for Minerals and Metals for 100% Renewable Scenarios," in *Achieving the Paris Climate Agreement Goals*, Sven Teske (ed.), 437–57 (Berlin: Springer, 2019). The authors assumed a world of 2050 that has a 100 percent renewable electricity supply with a (very modest) 6 percent of grid storage in lithium ion batteries, along with EVs making up only about half the global vehicle fleet. Requirements for metals would be much greater with more grid storage and full electrification of transportation.

183. Amit Katwala, "The Spiraling Environmental Cost of Our Lithium Battery Addiction," *Wired*, August 5, 2018.

184. Ibid.

185. Mike Ives, "Boom in Mining Rare Earths Poses Mounting Toxic Risks," *Yale Environment 360*, January 28, 2013.

186. Don Fitz, "How Green Is the Green New Deal?" *CounterPunch*, July 11, 2014.

187. Silja Halle (ed.), "From Conflict to Peacebuilding: The Role of Natural Resources and the Environment," United Nations Environment Program (2009), iisd.org/sites/default/files/publications/conflict_peacebuilding.pdf.

188. Tony Andrews, Bernarda Elizalde, Philippe Le Billon, Chang Hoon Oh, David Reyes, and Ian Thomson, "The Rise in Conflict Associated with Mining Operations: What Lies Beneath?" Canadian International Resources and Development Institute (2017), cirdi.ca/wp-content/uploads/2017/06/Conflict-Summary-060717.pdf.

189. Clare Church and Alec Crawford, "*Green Conflict Minerals*," International Institute for Sustainable Development (2018), iisd.org/sites/default/files/publications/green-conflict-minerals.pdf . According to IISD, between 30 and 75 percent of reserves of bauxite, cobalt, copper, lithium, molybdenum, nickel, silver, tellurium, titanium, and zinc are found in countries with impoverished governments prone to high levels of corruption. Greater than 75 percent of reserves of chromium, graphite, magnesium, selenium, tin, and the rare earth elements are in such countries. For rare earths, the figure is 94 percent. (Identification of fragile states is based on indicators related to economic stress, inequality, human displacement, oppression, human rights violations, weak rule of law, and intervention by other states.)

190. Allen White, "Solving the 10,000-Year-Old Problem of Agriculture: An Interview with Wes Jackson," *In These Times*, June 2016.

191. Richard York, phone interview with author, July 30, 2019.

192. Richard York and Shannon Elizabeth Bell, "Energy Transitions or Additions?: Why a Transition from Fossil Fuels Requires More than the Growth of Renewable Energy," *Energy Research & Social Science* 51(2019): 40–43.

193. U.S. Energy Information Agency, "Electric Power Monthly with Data for January 2019," March 2019, eia.gov/electricity/monthly/epm_table_grapher.php?t=epmt_1_1.Most of the decline in national emissions during that period was attributable to replacement of coal-fired power plants with ones that ran on natural gas. And even that trend may have been petering out; according to the Environmental Protection Agency, total carbon emissions from U.S. power plants increased in 2018. Iulia Gheorghiu, "EPA: Carbon Emissions from Power Plants Rose in 2018 amid Higher Electricity Demand," *Utility Dive*, February 21, 2019, utilitydive.com/news/epa-carbon-emissions-from-power-plants-rose-in-2018-amid-higher-electricit/548876/.

194. York and Bell, "Energy Transitions."

195. Robert Jackson, Corinne Le Quéré, R. M. Andrew, Josep Canadell, Jan Ivar Korsbakken, Zhu Liu, Glen Peters, and Bo Zheng, "Global Energy Growth Is Outpacing Decarbonization," *Environmental Research Letters* 13 (2018): 120401.

196. The idea of absolute decoupling—in which an economy's resource use or negative ecological impact declines at least as fast as its GDP increases—stands in contrast to "relative decoupling," in which the quantity of resource use or ecological impact per unit of GDP declines. Relative decoupling can happen, but it does not eliminate the negative effects of growth. See Tim Jackson and Peter Victor, "Unraveling the Claims for (and against) Green Growth," *Science* 366 (2019): 950–951.

197. Robert Fletcher and Crelis Rammelt. "Decoupling: A Key Fantasy of the Post-2015 Sustainable Development Agenda," *Globalizations* 14 (2017): 450–67.

198. Richard York and Julius McGee, "Does Renewable Energy Development Decouple Economic Growth from CO_2 Emissions?" *Socius* 3 (2017): 2378023116689098. For an extensive examination of so-called "green growth" and the dismal prospects for indefinite economic growth with commensurate reduction in resource use and greenhouse emissions, see Jason Hickel and Giorgos Kallis, "Is Green Growth Possible?, New Political Economy" (2019) DOI: 10.1080/13563467.2019.1598964. They cite James Ward, Paul Sutton, Adrian Werner, Robert Costanza, Steve Mohr, and Craig Simmons, "Is Decoupling GDP Growth from Environmental Impact Possible?" *PloS One* 11 (2016): e0164733. The authors show that improvements in resource efficiency will necessarily slow and eventually cease (because of physical limits, you can't produce goods with energy and resource use approaching zero), so as exponential economic growth proceeds, material and energy requirements cannot continue to fall, and will eventually rise. They conclude that "GDP ultimately cannot plausibly be decoupled from growth in material and energy use, demonstrating categorically that GDP growth cannot be sustained indefinitely. It is therefore misleading to develop growth-oriented policy around the expectation that decoupling is possible."

199. Timothée Parrique, Jonathan Barth, François Briens, Christian Kerschner, Alejo Kraus-Polk, Anna Kuokkanen, and Joachim Spangenberg, "Decoupling Debunked: Evidence and Arguments Against Green Growth as a Sole Strategy For Sustainability," European Environmental Bureau, 2019, eeb.org/library/decoupling-debunked. The European Union, for example, claims that its economies have managed to sever the link between economic growth and greenhouse emissions, based on a 13 percent decrease in emissions produced on European soil between 1990 and 2010; however, the continent's total greenhouse footprint, including imports, increased by 8 percent over those same years. There was no decoupling. In another study, Kyle Knight of the University of Alabama Huntsville and Juliet Schor of Boston College

showed that an apparent decoupling of GDP growth from emissions growth in twenty-nine high-income countries between 1991 and 2008 evaporated when consumption of imported goods was accounted for. See Kyle Knight and Juliet Schor, "Economic Growth and Climate Change: A Cross-National Analysis of Territorial and Consumption-Based Carbon Emissions in High-Income Countries," *Sustainability* 6 (2014): 3722–31.

200. Jackson and Victor, "Unraveling."

201. Xavier Labandeira, José Labeaga, and Xiral López-Otero, "A Meta-Analysis on the Price Elasticity of Energy Demand," *Energy Policy* 102 (2017): 549–68. Over the long term, the average decrease rises to 6 percent, but that doesn't help because the energy reductions required to meet immediate emissions goals must occur in the short term.

202. William Nordhaus, "Projections and Uncertainties About Climate Change in an Era of Minimal Climate Policies," *American Economic Journal: Economic Policy* 10 (2018): 333–60.

203. Juliet Schor, phone interview with author, July 23, 2019. Schor is author of the national bestseller *The Overworked American*.

204. James Boyce, "Carbon Pricing: Effectiveness and Equity," *Ecological Economics* 150 (2018): 52–61.

205. Note, however, that it's the limit on the total volume of permits, not the carbon price, that guarantees the reduction and elimination of fossil fuels on schedule. With a cap imposing the limit, the auction of permits would not even be needed to suppress consumption, yet the potentially steep inflation triggered by the auction would cause most families intense socioeconomic distress, rebate or no rebate. There would be plenty of complaining in the upper income brackets, but their consumption would remain high. As the national cap lowers to 75, then 50, then 25 percent of today's fuel supply, there's nothing to prevent the auction price from sailing into the thousands of dollars that the models predict if we employ a carbon price to keep us under 1.5°C of warming. The fossil-fuel extractors will keep happily passing their costs on to manufacturers, the transportation sector, and utilities. The original idea was that the escalating cost of fossil energy will prompt companies to switch to renewable energy. But in the decade or two when the steep emissions reductions have to happen, there will not be enough renewable capacity available to meet demand; therefore, the price of renewable energy will follow the steep upward trajectory of fossil fuels and the carbon price.

206. Henry Shue, "Subsistence Emissions and Luxury Emissions," *Law Policy* 15 (1993): 39–60.

207. Shaun Chamberlin, Larch Maxey, and Victoria Hurth, "Reconciling Scientific Reality with Realpolitik: Moving Beyond Carbon Pricing to TEQs—an Integrated, Economy-Wide Emissions Cap," *Carbon Management* 5 (2014): 411–27.

208. Stan Cox, *Any Way You Slice It: The Past, Present, and Future of Rationing* (New York: The New Press, 2013), 38–41, 247–50; Daniel Kahneman, Jack Knetsch, and Richard Thaler, "Fairness and the Assumptions of Economics," *Journal of Business* 59 (1986): s285–s300; Ernst Fehr and Klaus Schmidt, "A Theory of Fairness, Competition, and Cooperation," *Quarterly Journal of Economics* 114 (1999): 817–68; Ernst Fehr and Jean-Robert Tyran, "Institutions and Reciprocal Fairness," *Nordic Journal of Political Economy* 23 (1996): 133–44; David Savage and Benno Torgler, "Perceptions of Fairness and Allocation Systems," *Economic Analysis and Policy* 40 (2010): 229–48; Yochai Benkler, "Law, Policy, and Cooperation," in *Government and Markets: Toward a New Theory of Regulation*, ed. Edward Balleisen and David Moss (New York: Cambridge University Press, 2009), 101–12.

209. United Nations Environment Programme, "The Production Gap: The Discrepancy Between Countries' Planned Fossil Fuel Production and Global Production Levels Consistent with Limiting Warming to 1.5°C or 2°C," 2019, productiongap.org/.

210. Richard York, phone interview with author, July 30, 2019.

211. Ted Nace, Lydia Plante, and James Browning, "Pipeline Bubble: North America Is Betting Over $1 Trillion on a Risky Fossil Infrastructure Boom," *Global Energy Monitor*, April 2019.

212. Oliver Milman, "North American Drilling Boom Threatens Big Blow to Climate Efforts, Study Finds," *The Guardian*, April 25, 2019. Another recent report found that if all such infrastructure worldwide—existing, under construction and planned—is operated through its expected lifetime, the resulting emissions alone will blow through the global limits that would avert 1.5 or even 2 °C of warming. Dan Tong, Qiang Zhang, Yixuan Zheng, Ken Caldeira, Christine Shearer, Chaopeng Hong, Yue Qin, and Steven Davis, "Committed Emissions from Existing Energy Infrastructure Jeopardize 1.5° C Climate Target," *Nature* (2019): doi.org/10.1038/s41586-019-1364-3.

213. Janet Redman, Kelly Trout, Alex Doukas, and Ken Bossong, "Dirty Energy Dominance: Dependent on Denial," *Oil Change International*, October 3, 2017, priceofoil.org/2017/10/03/dirty-energy-dominance-us-subsidies.

214. Several contenders for the 2020 Democratic presidential nomination, including Elizabeth Warren, Bernie Sanders, and Kirsten Gillibrand, signed onto the "Keep It in The Ground Act," a bill introduced by Senator Jeff Merkley that would block new oil, coal and gas leases on public land and waters.

215. Matthew Merrill, Benjamin Sleeter, Philip Freeman, Jinxun Liu, Peter Warwick, and Bradley Reed, "Federal Lands Greenhouse Gas Emissions and Sequestration in the United States: Estimates for 2005–14," U.S. Geological Survey, 2018, pubs.er.usgs.gov/publication/sir20185131.

216. Michael Lazarus and Harro van Asselt, "Fossil Fuel Supply and Climate Policy: Exploring the Road Less Taken," *Climatic Change* 150 (2018): 1–13.

217. Fergus Green and Richard Denniss, "Cutting with Both Arms of the Scissors: The Economic and Political Case for Restrictive Supply-Side Climate Policies," *Climatic Change* 150 (2018): 73–87.

218. Richard York, interview with the author, July 30, 2019.

219. Keep It in the Ground, keepitintheground.org.

220. Julie Ayling and Neil Gunningham, "Non-State Governance and Climate Policy: The Fossil Fuel Divestment Movement," *Climate Policy* 17 (2017): 131–49.

221. 350.org, "Major Milestone: 1000+ Divestment Commitments," go fossilfree.org/major-milestone-1000-divestment-commitments/.

222. Tyler Hansen and Robert Pollin, "Economics and Climate Justice Activism: Assessing the Fossil Fuel Divestment Movement," Political Economy Research Institute, Working Paper Series No. 462, April 2018, wrongkindof green.org/wp-content/uploads/2018/11/Economics-and-Climate-Justice -Activism-Assessing-the-Fossil-Fuel-Divestment-Movement.pdf.

223. Ayling, J. and Gunningham, "Non-State Governance."

224. Patrick Moriarty and Damon Honnery, "A Human Needs Approach to Reducing Atmospheric Carbon," *Energy Policy* 38 (2010): 695–700.

225. Eleanor Boyle, "The climate crisis is like a world war. So let's talk about rationing," *Globe and Mail*, December 14, 2019.

226. Benjamin Neimark, Oliver Belcher, and Patrick Bigger, "US Military Is a Bigger Polluter than as Many as 140 Countries–Shrinking This War Machine Is a Must," *The Conversation*, June 24, 2019.

227. Ilona Otto, Kyoung Mi Kim, Nika Dubrovsky, and Wolfgang Lucht, "Shift the Focus from the Super-Poor to the Super-Rich," *Nature Climate Change* 9 (2019): 82–83.

228. World Bank, "World Development Indicators," datacatalog.world bank.org/dataset/world-development-indicators.

229. The Human Development Index, expressed on a zero-to-one scale, is a composite of three indicators: life expectancy at birth, years of education, and income. It is often adjusted for inequality. United Nations Development Program, "Inequality-Adjusted Human Development Report," hdr.undp.org/ en/composite/IHDI.

230. Richard Easterlin, Laura Angelescu McVey, Malgorzata Switek, Onnicha Sawangfa, and Jacqueline Smith Zweig, "The Happiness–Income Paradox Revisited," *Proceedings of the National Academy of Sciences* 107 (2010): 22463–468.

231. Jason Hickel, "The Sustainable Development Index: Measuring the Ecological Efficiency of Human Development in the Anthropocene," *Ecological Economics* 167 (2020): 106331. The SDI is on a zero-to-one scale. The four mentioned nations that have about one-fourth of U.S energy consumption have an average SDI of 0.64. Those with about half of U.S. energy consumption average 0.34 in SDI. The United States' SDI is 0.18.

232. Jason Hickel, "Inequality and the Ecological Transition," January 14, 2019, jasonhickel.org/blog/2019/1/14/inequality-and-the-ecological-transition.

233. Erzo Luttmer, "Neighbors as Negatives: Relative Earnings and Well-Being," *Quarterly Journal of Economics* 120 (2005): 963–1002; James Coleman, "Social Capital in the Creation of Human Capital," *American Journal of Sociology* 94 (1988): s95–s120; John Helliwell and Robert Putnam, "The Social Context of Well-Being," *Philosophical Transactions of the Royal Society of London B* 359 (2004): 1435–46; Thorstein Veblen, *The Theory of the Leisure Class* (New York: Modern Library, 1931).

234. Don Fitz, "A Deep Green Alternative," *CounterPunch*, July 26, 2013.

235. See, for example, this analysis published at the peak of the 2000s boom: Jared Bernstein and Lawrence Mishel, "Economy's Gains Fail to Reach Most Workers' Paychecks," Economic Policy Institute Briefing Paper 195, August 30, 2007, epi.org/publication/bp195.

236. Giorgos Kallis, "Radical Dematerialization and Degrowth," *Philosophical Transactions of the Royal Society A: Mathematical, Physical and Engineering Sciences* 375 (2017): 20160383.

237. Anna Coote, "10 Reasons for a Shorter Working Week," New Economics Foundation, July 29, 2014, neweconomics.org/2014/07/10-reasons -for-a-shorter-working-week.

238. Giorgos Kallis, Vasilis Kostakis, Steffen Lange, Barbara Muraca, Susan Paulson, and Matthias Schmelzer, "Research on Degrowth," *Annual Review of Environment and Resources* 43 (2018): 291–316.

239. Giorgio Kallis, *Degrowth* (Agenda: Newcastle-Upon-Tyne, 2018), 124–25.

240. Ernest Callenbach, *Ecotopia: Thirtieth Anniversary Edition* (Berkeley: Banyan Tree, 2004).

241. In January, 2020, thirty-five years after Callenbach envisioned a traffic-free Market Street, the city of San Francisco began enforcing a prohibition on all private and ride-share vehicles along a two-mile stretch of the downtown thoroughfare. Amy Hollyfield and Kate Larsen, "Private Vehicle Ban Begins on Market Street in San Francisco," *ABC7 San Francisco*, January 30, 2020, abc7news.com/5887897/.

242. Ibid., 29. Callenbach continues: "Indeed this is probably a major Ecotopian myth; keep hearing references to what Indians would and wouldn't do in a given situation. . . . But what matters most is the aspiration to live in balance with nature, 'walk lightly on the land,' treat the earth as a mother."

243. Ibid., 98–100.

244. Scott Timberg, "A '70s Cult Novel Is Relevant Again." *New York Times*, December 12, 2008.

245. Ibid.

246. Ibid.; the Mann quote is from Twitter.

247. Joseph Nevins, "Mitigating Climate Disaster Will Require Both Systemic and Lifestyle Changes," *Truthout*, April 17, 2017.

248. Wes Jackson and Robert Jensen, "Let's Get 'Creaturely': A New Worldview Can Help Us Face Ecological Crises," *Resilience*, April 3, 2019.

249. Richard York, "Environmental Consequences of Moral Disinhibition," *Socius* 3 (2017): 2378023117719612.

250. Laura Berry, of The Climate Mobilization, email interview by author, August 26, 2019; on the symbolism of Los Angeles, see Mike Davis, *Ecology of Fear: Los Angeles and the Imagination of Disaster* (New York: Vintage, 1999).

251. Charlie Gardner and Claire Wordley, "Scientists Must Act on Our Own Warnings to Humanity," *Nature Ecology & Evolution* 3 (2019): 1271–72.

252. Linley Sanders, "Calexit: The 'Yes California' Independence Bid Returns on Valentine's Day to Divorce America," *Newsweek*, January 27, 2018.

253. Emily Holden, "Sanders and Ocasio-Cortez Move to Declare Climate Crisis Official Emergency," *The Guardian*, July 8, 2019.

254. Larry Edwards and Stan Cox, "Cap and Adapt: A Failsafe Approach to the Climate Emergency," *Resilience*, August 28, 2019.

255. UNEP, "Emissions Gap Report"; To emphasize: The annual reductions must be a percentage of the *initial* annual fuel use. If we were to instead prescribe a percentage of the previous year's use (in the way that, for example, GDP growth is typically expressed as a percentage of the previous year's GDP), fossil fuel use would decline far too slowly and would never reach zero.

256. The term "cap and cope," like "cap and adapt," was Larry Edwards's idea.

257. Jonathan Franzen, "What If We Stopped Pretending the Climate Apocalypse Can Be Stopped?" *New Yorker*, September 8, 2019; Wallace Wells, *The Uninhabitable Earth*.

258. Avichai Scher, "'Climate Grief': The Growing Emotional Toll of Climate Change," NBC News, December 24, 2018, nbcnews.com/health/mental-health/climate-grief-growing-emotional-toll-climate-change-n946751.

259. Robert Jensen, "With a World 'On Fire,' We Need More Than Inspiration," *CommonDreams*, September 17, 2019, www.commondreams.org/views/2019/09/17/danger-inspiration-review-fire-burning-case-green-new-deal.

260. Michelle Goldberg, "Democracy Grief Is Real," *New York Times*, December 13, 2019.

261. The ecosphere includes the biosphere but is more comprehensive, encompassing the Earth's soils, waters, atmosphere, and other inanimate entities that are components of ecosystems. See Wes Jackson, Aubrey Streit Krug, Bill Vitek, and Robert Jensen, "Transforming human life on our home planet, perennially," *The Ecological Citizen* 2 (2018): 3–46.

262. Big Petroleum fought hard for decades to deny that human-induced greenhouse warming was occurring, even as their own experts were telling them

it was a growing threat. See Emily Holden, "Exxon Sowed Doubt about Climate Crisis, House Democrats Hear in Testimony," *The Guardian*, October 23, 2019.

263. Ilhan Omar, "It's Time to End the Affordable Housing Crisis Once and for All," *Minneapolis Star Tribune*, November 22, 2019.

264. Bill Moyer, Patrick Mazza, and J. Craig Thorpe, *Solutionary Rail: A People-Powered Campaign to Electrify America's Railroads and Open Corridors to a Clean Energy Future* (Vashon, WA: Backbone Campaign, 2016); see solution-aryrail.org.

265. Ezra Silk, "The Climate Mobilization Victory Plan," initial publication in August 2016, revision by Kaela Bamberger published in March 2019, drive.google.com/file/d/0Bze7GXvI3ywrSGxYWDVXM3hVUm8/view.

266. The Tradable Energy Quotas system (TEQs) differs from Edwards's and my cap-and-adapt system by allocating all energy sources on the basis of their relative emissions rather than by physical quantity. That would be the preferred way to go if the goal were to reduce total emissions by substituting one fuel for another. At this late date, however, our goal is to free ourselves from *all* fossil fuels, and the simplest way to do that is to reduce them all at the same rate. If we allocate and ration based on emissions instead, a big part of the reduction in the early years would result from simply substituting natural gas for coal and liquid fuels. That would trigger a scaled-up fracking boom and would also dramatically increase emissions of methane, a powerful greenhouse gas. Already, a global buildup of natural gas–fired electric capacity is threatening to lock in big future emissions increases. See Nicholas Kusnetz, "Natural Gas Rush Drives a Global Rise in Fossil Fuel Emissions," *Inside Climate News*, December 3, 2019. We would also end up building new fossil-fuel-dependent infrastructure at a time when we need to be tearing it down. And having picked the low-hanging fruit, we would leave the much more difficult withdrawal from natural gas for last. Edwards and I, rather than relying on an auction to allocate fossil fuels among buyers as with TEQs, would have the sellers (which with nationalization would be public entities) decide how resources could be allocated to serve the public interest.

267. Larry Edwards, email to author, February 21, 2019.

268. Amy Bentley, *Eating for Victory: Food Rationing and the Politics of Domesticity* (Champaign: University of Illinois Press, 1998), 21.

269. Tom DiChristopher, "Alexandria Ocasio-Cortez Floats 70% Tax on Wealthy to Pay for 'Green New Deal,'" CNBC, January 4, 2019.

270. Yeva Nersisyan and L. Randall Wray, "How to Pay for the Green New Deal," *Levy Economics Institute Working Papers Series* 931 (2019).

271. "In Summary: The Green New Deal," *New Consensus*, February 2019, newconsensus.com/wp-content/uploads/2019/02/new_consensus_gnd_2_pager.pdf.

272. Jeff Stein and David Weigel, "Ocasio-Cortez retracts erroneous information about Green New Deal backed by 2020 Democratic candidates," *Washington Post*, February 11, 2019. The fact sheet was taken offline soon after

being posted and can be found today only on right-wing websites attacking the Green New Deal. The FAQ had been attacked immediately (most prominently by the @realdonaldtrump Twitter account) for its jokey references to, for example, getting rid of "farting cows" and airplanes. But deep reductions in meat consumption and air travel will indeed be required if greenhouse emissions are to be reduced at the required rate.

273. Recall the study James Ward et al., "Is Decoupling GDP Growth from Environmental Impact Possible?", discussed in Chapter 3, and the authors' conclusion that increases in efficiency slow down over time, while GDP growth speeds up, and therefore, "GDP ultimately cannot plausibly be decoupled from growth in material and energy use, demonstrating categorically that GDP growth cannot be sustained indefinitely."

274. Naomi Klein, *On Fire: The Burning Case for a Green New Deal* (New York: Simon and Schuster, 2019), 264.

275. Richard Reeves, *Dream Hoarders: How the American Upper Middle Class Is Leaving Everyone Else in the Dust* (Washington, D.C.: Brookings, 2017).

276. Kate Raworth, *Doughnut Economics: Seven Ways to Think Like a 21st-Century Economist* (White River Junction, VT: Chelsea Green, 2017).

277. J. Bricker, L. Dettling, A. Henriques, J. Hsu, K. Moore, J. Sabelhaus, and J. Krimmel, "Changes in U.S. Family Finances from 2010 to 2013: Evidence from the Survey of Consumer Finances" (Vol. 100). Board of Governors of the Federal Reserve System, federalreserve.gov/pubs/bulletin/2014/pdf/scf14.pdf.

278. U.S. Census Bureau, "Wealth, Asset Ownership, & Debt of Households," 2011, census.gov/data/tables/2011/demo/wealth/wealth-asset-ownership.html.

279. U.S. Census Bureau, "Historical Income Tables: Households," undated, census.gov/data/tables/time-series/demo/income-poverty/historical-income-households.html.

280. Craig Welch, "A Way Forward," *National Geographic*, October 15, 2016, nationalgeographic.com/climate-change/carbon-free-power-grid/article.html.

281. Winona La Duke, "Prophecy of the Seventh Fire: Choosing the Path That Is Green," Thirty-Seventh Annual E.F. Schumacher Lecture, November 2017, centerforneweconomics.org/publications/prophecy-of-the-seventh-fire-choosing-the-path-that-is-green/.

282. John Bellamy Foster, Hannah Holleman, and Brett Clark, "Imperialism in the Anthropocene," *Monthly Review*, July–August 2019.

283. Ibid.

284. The opposite is now happening; Ibid.

285. Patrick Moriarty, email interview by author, August 30, 2019.

286. John Dearing et al., "Safe and Just Operating Spaces for Regional Social-Ecological Systems," *Global Environmental Change* 28 (2014): 227–38.

287. IPCC, "Climate Change and Land," August, 2019, ipcc.ch/report/srccl.

288. Timothy Crews, "Closing the Gap between Grasslands and Grain Agriculture," *Kansas Journal of Law and Public Policy* 26 (2016): 274–96.

289. Martin Cames, et al., "How Additional Is the Clean Development Mechanism?," Oeko-Institut EV CLIMA. B 3 (2016), verifavia.com/uploads/files/clean_dev_mechanism_en.pdf.

290. James Temple, "Whoops! California's Carbon Offsets Program Could Extend the Life of Coal Mines," *MIT Technology Review*, August 26, 2019; Barbara Haya et al., "Managing Uncertainty in Carbon Offsets: Insights from California's Standardized Approach," Stanford Law School ENRLP Program Working Paper, Stanford, CA, August, 2019, www-cdn.law.stanford.edu/wp-content/uploads/2015/03/Managing-Uncertainty-in-Carbon-Offsets-SLS-Working-Paper.pdf.

291. Lisa Song, "An (Even More) Inconvenient Truth: Why Carbon Credits for Forest Preservation May Be Worse Than Nothing," *ProPublica*, May 22, 2019.

292. "ICA Youth Delegation demand non-market climate solutions and Indigenous rights in Article 6," Indigenous Climate Action, December 5, 2019, www.indigenousclimateaction.com/post/ica-youth-delegation-demand-non-market-climate-solutions-and-indigenous-rights-in-article-6.

293. Kevin Anderson, "The Inconvenient Truth of Carbon Offsets," *Nature News* 484 (2012): 7.

294. Shoibal Chakravarty, Ananth Chikkatur, Heleen De Coninck, Stephen Pacala, Robert Socolow, and Massimo Tavoni, "Sharing Global CO_2 Emission Reductions Among One Billion High Emitters," *Proceedings of the National Academy of Sciences* 29 (2009): 11884–88.

295. Lukas Meyer and Dominic Roser, "Distributive Justice and Climate Change: The Allocation of Emission Rights," *Analyse & Kritik* 28 (2006): 223–49.

296. Feasta, "Cap and Share," feasta.org/category/documents/projects/cap-and-share; Justin Kenrick, "Presenting Cap and Share to a Citizens' Assembly in the Scottish Parliament," Feasta blog, February 3, 2019, www.feasta.org/2019/02/03/report-on-presenting-cap-and-share-to-a-citizens-assembly-in-the-scottish-parliament.

297. Michael Hoexter, "Living in the Web of Soft Climate Denial," *New Economic Perspectives*, September 7, 2016.

298. Rupert Read, "What Is New in Our Time: The Truth in 'PostTruth'," *Nordic Wittgenstein Review* Special Issue (2019): 81–96.

299. La Duke, "Prophecy."

ABOUT THE AUTHOR

STAN COX is the author of many books, including *Losing Our Cool: Uncomfortable Truths About Our Air-Conditioned World (and Finding New Ways to Get Through the Summer)*; *Any Way You Slice It: The Past, Present and Future of Rationing*; and *How the World Breaks: Life in Catastrophe's Path, from the Caribbean to Siberia* (co-authored with Paul Cox). Cox has a Ph.D. in plant genetics from Iowa State University. During a career first in the U.S. Department  of Agriculture and now at The Land Institute, he has authored more than 90 peer-reviewed scientific papers. Since 2003, he has written for a general readership about the economic and political roots of the global ecological crisis. His writing has appeared in the *New York Times, Washington Post, Los Angeles Times, Hartford Courant, Atlanta Journal-Constitution, Baltimore Sun, Denver Post, Kansas City Star, Arizona Republic, The New Republic, The Guardian, Al Jazeera, Salon,* and *Dissent,* and in local publications spanning forty-three U.S. states. In 2012, *The Atlantic* named Cox their "Readers' Choice Brave Thinker" for his critique of air conditioning.

ALSO AVAILABLE IN THE OPEN MEDIA SERIES

Storming the Wall
Climate Change, Migration, and Homeland Security
By Todd Miller

Loaded
A Disarming History of the Second Amendment
By Roxanne Dunbar-Ortiz

United States of Distraction
Media Manipulation in Post-Truth America
(And What We Can Do About It)
By Mickey Huff and Nolan Higdon

Breaking Through Power
By Ralph Nader

American Nightmare
Facing the Challenge of Fascism
By Henry A. Giroux

I Couldn't Even Imagine That They Would Kill Us
An Oral History of the Attacks Against the Students of Ayotzinapa
By John Gibler, Foreword by Ariel Dorfman

Have Black Lives Ever Mattered?
By Mumia Abu-Jamal

The Meaning of Freedom
By Angela Y. Davis, Foreword by Robin D.G. Kelley

CITY LIGHTS BOOKS | OPEN MEDIA SERIES
arm yourself with information